Rothwell Castle and Medieval Life

By
Rothwell and District Historical Society

Published by RDHS Press
1 St Georges Crescent
Rothwell
Leeds LS26 0RN

Typeset, originated and printed by Heritage House Press.
19 South Ridge, Kippax. Leeds. LS25 7NE

ISBN 0 9539334 1 5

First Published 2006

Rothwell Castle and Medieval Life

By
Rothwell and District Historical Society

Contents

LHi
Local Heritage *initiative*

Heritage Lottery Fund

Nationwide

The Countryside Agency

ENGLISH HERITAGE

PRO REGE ET LEGE

LEEDS
CITY COUNCIL

West Yorkshire
Archaeology Service
Advisory Service

Education Leeds

Acknowledgments

THIS BOOK HAS BEEN MADE POSSIBLE through a grant made by Local Heritage Initiative (LHF) and Nationwide Building Society. Special thanks must go to them for believing in our project. Also, special thanks go to the other organisations that have given generously to this project.

Brian Walker, Leeds City Council, James Normington, Education Leeds, West Yorkshire Archaeology Service (WYAS), the School Children of Rothwell, Bret Harrison, Christopher Whittock, Dave Weldrake, Liz Weldrake, Stuart Wrathmell, Susan Bulmer, Margaret Wright, David Rains, Alec Sawyer, Members of Rothwell and District Historical Society, Rothwell Library, West Yorkshire Archive Service, John Prudoe, Emma Carter, Jane Haigh, Fred Duff, Richard Taylor, John Thorpe, Julian Healey, Keith Emerick, English Heritage, Lord Mowbray, Segrave and Stourton, Shelley Signs, Michael Ashley, Mike Ball, Rothwell Rotary, Rothwell in Bloom, British Library, South Leeds City Learning Centre (CLC), Jan Symonds, *Rothwell Record*, *Wakefield Express*, Stephen Ward, and to any other organisation or individual who has contributed to the project.

Thanks go to Ian Sanderson whose knowledge of archaeology and general advice has been invaluable.

Special thanks go to Steve Burt, whose vision, expertise and commitment to this project has been an inspiration to

Rothwell and District Historical Society. To Howard Bicknell, Mike Parsons and Heritage House Press, our knights in shining armour. The committee of Rothwell Castle Project would all like to express our sincere, deep felt thanks.

To the following people we express our sincere gratitude for their commitment, loyalty and sheer hard work: Pat Edwards, Audrey Rains, Norma Sawyer, Eric Wright, Mary Fleet and Simon Bulmer: thanks for all those meetings and nights writing and rewriting this book.

Editor's note: Because so many aspects of medieval life were inextricably interwoven, such as religion with agriculture, hunting with food, repetition of facts within different sections of the book is unavoidable. It was felt that to omit references from any chapter for this reason alone would interfere with its overall scope.

This book is dedicated to the common men and women whose lives in medieval Rothwell helped mould and create the village and whose voices can still be heard through ancient texts. Hopefully this book has, many centuries later, given those voices a chance to speak again.

Sources of Illustrations and photographs

ROTHWELL AND DISTRICT HISTORICAL SOCIETY would like to thank to the following bodies, societies and individuals who have kindly granted permission to reproduce their material.

British Library

Eric Wright

David Rains

West Yorkshire Archaeology Survey

Other contributors are noted with their pictures

Some illustrations used are of unknown copyright or it has expired

Special thanks go to West Yorkshire Archaeology Service for permitting us to reproduce their written work contained in this book.

Front cover illustration:
King John Hunting - 14th century illustration
© British Library

Foreword

IF QUEEN ELIZABETH II WERE TO VISIT ROTHWELL TODAY it would be viewed as a remarkable, exciting and memorable event. Yet in the medieval period Kings of England regularly visited the hunting park of Rothwell Haigh and lodged in the nearby castle. Sadly there is only one isolated stump of masonry left in a field near the church to remind us of this important historic site.

Fortunately a recent resistivity survey revealed that just beneath the surface are the extensive remains of structures which included the Great Hall, a manor house, brewhouse, bakery, chapel, smithy and at least one barn.

So why was it constructed here? Who built it? What did it look like? What would it have been like to work in Rothwell over eight hundred years ago? So many questions!

This wonderful book has been written by members of Rothwell and District Historical Society. Its aim is to share with the general reader the fruits of their research and to paint a picture of what it must have been like to live here during the medieval period.

For many, this was the first time they had ever undertaken such a task and it must have been daunting to be faced with a blank piece of paper and wonder how they were going to interest their friends and neighbours!

I think that the contributors are to be congratulated on managing to tell a very coherent story of life in Rothwell that gives the reader a flavour of the lifestyle of medieval 'Rodillers'.

The breadth of this work is remarkable - from castle to market, diet to health and hunting to religion. This book will advance residents' knowledge of the area and hopefully encourage others to research into the history of one of the most important medieval sites in West Yorkshire.

Steve Burt
Collections Director
Royal Armouries, Leeds
December 2006

Introduction

By Simon Bulmer

THE POSSIBILITY OF A PROJECT to investigate Rothwell Castle was first discussed in the office of the then leader of Leeds City Council, Brian Walker. It was in his office at the Civic Hall, while discussing the plans for the Rothwell Millennium Group (R2K), that the castle was first mentioned.

Brian had accumulated a large dossier on the castle over the years, with much correspondence to and from English Heritage and other organisations, with a view to setting up a project to formally investigate the site, but alas this had never got off the ground.

I had made a mental note of what was said that day way back in the late 1990s.

The seed grew after a series of events in 2001.

The first was another opportunity for me to work with Albert Brown on his unpublished work about the history of Rothwell Castle, which highlighted the need for further research.

About the same time, Steve Burt, then the Manager of South Leeds CLC, was asked to write the Rothwell Colliery Educational Pack to celebrate the opening of the Rothwell Country Park.

Steve asked for the assistance of the Rothwell and District Historical Society and has been working alongside the society ever since!

An initial meeting of the Rothwell Castle Project Committee was held in May 2002. It was at this meeting that the concept of the project was brought together.

With the completion of the grant application to Local Heritage Initiative (LHF), it was a big 'thumbs up' for the project to start.

We had already set up a number of archaeological investigations on the pastures surrounding the castle site through South Leeds CLC, Education Leeds and West Yorkshire Archaeological Service. This gave the local children a fantastic opportunity to experience archaeology at first hand.

The first excavations took place in the summer of 2002, after a geophysical survey identified possible archaeological sites on the pastures. These investigations continued for three years as the Rothwell Castle Project gathered momentum.

The dedication and hard work of all those involved with the project has ensured that the outcomes have been beneficial for the community of Rothwell, as It will enlighten and educate those who take pride in Rothwell's fascinating history.

Simon Bulmer
Chair of Rothwell Castle Project
December 2006

1. Pre-Domesday Rothwell

THE DOMESDAY BOOK is the earliest written record of Rothwell that we have been able to find, therefore we can only use archaeological information to paint a picture of pre-1086 Rothwell.

The earliest physical evidence found is an example of two Bronze Age pot urns dug up in a garden in Wood Lane in May 1949. There was evidence of cremated human remains in the urns, which is now in the collection of Leeds City Council Museums. This does not necessarily indicate that Rothwell and its surrounding area was occupied at this time, but could have been an isolated burial of a group passing through the area.

We have much more evidence of Roman occupation within Rothwell and the surrounding villages. In 1607 a

A coin of the Roman emperor Alexander Severus (193 – 211AD) similar to the ones that were found at Lingwell gate in the 19th century.

A coin of the Roman emperor Hadrian (117 –138AD) similar to the ones that were found at Lingwell gate in the 19th century.

number of Roman coins was found at Lingwell Gate, as was a great number of coins and moulds picked up in 1814 and 1815 in a field by a local girl.

On another occasion, in 1821, a large number of coins, coin moulds and crucibles was found and yet seventy more coin moulds and a funnel found, again at Lingwell Gate. These were presented to the Leeds Philosopher Society in 1829. Some of these finds can be dated to the reigns of Hadrian (CE. 117-138) and Alexander Serverus (CE. 222-235) and were doubtless struck near to where they were found.

In 1823 workmen found a stone coffin while cutting a new roadway on Bell Hill. This coffin, made of grit stone, measured 1.5 metres in length and contained a number of beads of differing sizes, materials and colours, which led to the speculation that it had contained a female of Roman origin.

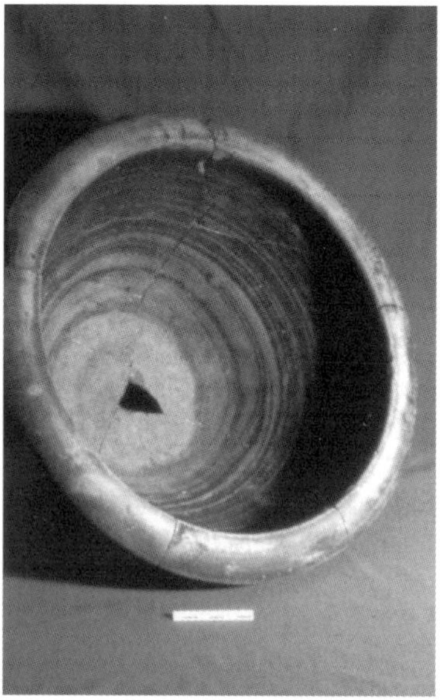

One of the clay bowls that was excavated from the 4th century Roman well.

©West Yorkshire Archaeology Service (WYAS) 1977

In 1870, while the foundations for a brewery at Carlton were being dug, a Roman horseshoe was found.

These two discoveries lead us to believe that there were probably a number of roman roads through the area.

It was common practice to bury the dead in private fields or gardens next to a highway as a reminder to passers-by of their own mortality.

A so-called Roman Camp was found in the 19th century, located in Lofthouse Hall Park, consisting of a rampart, ditch and central quadrangle. The ditch enclosed approximately 2000 square yards.

A Roman well was discovered in land adjacent to Rothwell Colliery (Fanny Pit) in 1977. After extensive excavation it was found to yield many dateable finds at the bottom, from 4th century pottery to wooden items such as a spade and bowls. Many different animal bones were also found.

At the time a human skull was found but archaeologists thought that this could have been a burial site unrelated to the Roman period.

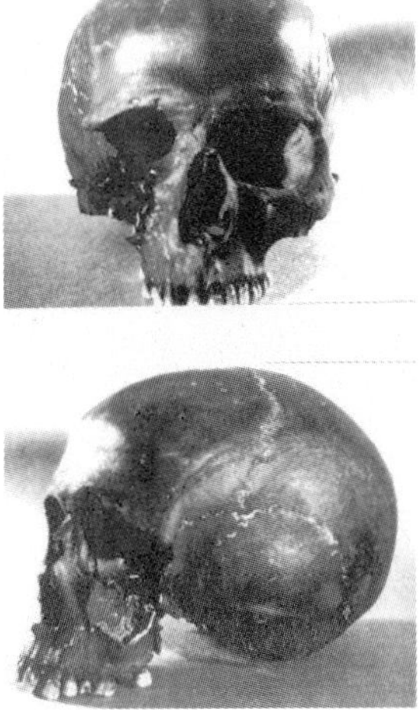

The human skull that was found at the bottom of the 4th century Roman well.

©West Yorkshire Archaeology Service (WYAS) 1977

There was evidence, even though much disturbed, of a possible farm settlement encircled by a ditch, which would have been typical of that time.

We know virtually nothing of life in Rothwell between the Roman period and the Anglo Saxon settlement that undoubtedly existed, one assumes on, or very near the current site of the medieval manor house. The only evidence for this settlement is from the Domesday Book of 1086 in which five wooden or stone halls one in Rothwell, Lofthouse, Carlton, Thorpe on the Hill and Middleton are recorded. We believe these are written down in order of importance, as are the Anglo Saxon Thanes (Lords), Harold at Rothwell, Barth at Lofthouse, Alric at Carlton and Stenulf at Middleton and Thorpe.

This leaves Ilbert de Lacy, who owned all the land about, which, in reality, meant that the Saxon Thanes at this time were tenants and not landowners in their own right.

All this is pure conjecture and is open to question until further evidence comes to light.

2. Why build a castle at Rothwell?

CASTLES WERE HUGELY IMPORTANT throughout the unstable early history of our island nation. They guarded the highways of commerce, protected the monarch and the ruling elite and defended the nation in times of national emergency. A castle was not just a fortress and a military base; it was a home, an administrative centre, and a physical representation of power and wealth.

The castle was a multi-function building, the lynch-pin of society for almost 500 years. Without castles, and all they represented, the Normans might have been wiped off the face of the British Isles.

Thanks to their reliance on castles the Normans were able to successfully conquer England, Scotland, Ireland and, last but not least, Wales.

Each castle was different, incorporating different ideas, different designs and materials. Designs changed throughout the British castle-building period (1066-1450s). They differed in size and scale. Improvements were incorporated as weapons and warfare evolved. Some were grand palatial piles, like the Tower of London, others were much smaller, nothing more than timber towers with timber palisades. Others evolved from timber castles into stone fortresses with a stone *Donjon* (Keep), moats and outer walls. Some developed into small, compact, fortified manor houses, built as homes rather than fortresses.

The years following the Norman Invasion of England were extremely dangerous. The Normans were an invading force and the local population was hostile. The uprisings in the North of England increased the fear of

Northerners by the new Norman hierarchy and were vigorously put down in campaigns known as the 'Harrying of the North'.

It should be remembered that the Norman Conquest brought great changes to the whole country.

Norman lords replaced the old Anglo-Saxon nobility. People, who for hundreds of years had worked for, fought for and respected generations of the same local family of Earls now had new masters. Not only was there a change of personalities, these new lords spoke a different language, Anglo-French, which differed from the local dialects. These major changes created a gap between the local people and their new masters.

Following the Harrying of the North the Normans realised that there was a need to control the North of England. Its people were hostile to the King and the newly arrived nobility. There was no quick way of accessing the North from their southern base so any future rebellion would have to be dealt with at a local level.

Benefiting from their experience in Normandy, it was not surprising the Normans introduced castles to establish their authority. The castle had proved most successful in providing a strong defensive home to the members of the nobility. It combined living quarters with defensive features and administrative space. The advantage of the castle is that it could be built anywhere, on any type of terrain.

Castles generally took one of two forms: the *motte-and-bailey* and the Enclosure castle. Motte-and-bailey castles were compact and could be built very quickly, in fact William the Conqueror brought a 'flat-pack' castle with him from Normandy when he invaded.

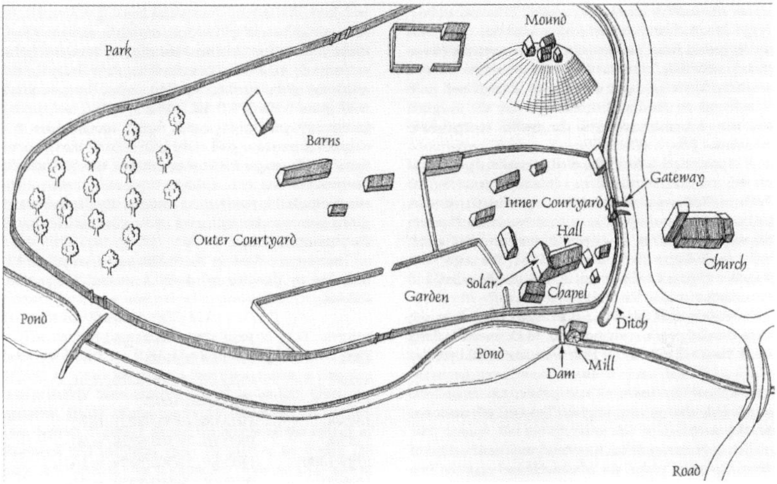

An artist's impression of what the fortified manor might have look like in the 14th century.

In the 50 years following the Battle of Hastings in 1066 the simple motte-and-bailey castle became popular. It was relatively cheap and easy to build, rather like the 'prefab' houses of the 1940s and 1950s. The wooden castle was vulnerable to fire and it was not always suitable in all areas. This led to the development of many different styles, built in wood and stone, usually incorporating geographical features.

A good example of this is Richmond Castle in North Yorkshire, built on the cliff overlooking the River Swale. Richmond is an early example of the enclosure castle built in stone in the late 11th century. There was no need to build a high mound here as the cliff overlooking the river already provided a natural defensive position. The Hall (now known as Scolland's Hall) was the centre of the castle and this was then 'enclosed' by a simple wall, hence the term, 'enclosure' castle.

The motte-and-bailey consisted of two distinct areas: the mound (or *motte*) and an enclosed area below the motte called the bailey.

The tower on the bailey was not used as a residence but as a defensive position. We know this by looking at other examples of motte-and-bailey castles.

The remains of the castle at Middleham, now known as William's Hill, show a fine example of early Norman castle building. The timber superstructure of the castle has long since disappeared but the earthworks remain. The earthworks are set high above the valley giving a clear view across the countryside below. This allowed the occupants of the castle to keep watch over the countryside and guard against invasions, revolt and rebellions. The prominence of the motte-and-bailey castle at William's Hill also acted as a constant reminder to the local population that the Normans now ran the country. The castle represented social and geographical superiority over the peasantry.

The steep slope and ditch at the base of the motte make the position very difficult to attack. The steep contours of the man-made motte at Williams Hill are undoubtedly similar to the ones that existed at Rothwell.

These defensive features (steep sloping motte, ditch and a tower) allowed the garrison strong positions to retire to should they be attacked. Castles did not house hundreds of men, as feature films would have us believe. The strength of the castle was in its design. It was a strong structure and could be defended by as few as five or six men.

The revenues that the lords brought in from the manor would have to cover the cost of repairing and upgrading of the castle. A large garrison would need to be fed, clothed and paid. Any men who did protect the castle would undoubtedly have had a second role. It was not uncommon for Medieval knights to turn up on the battlefield with ten men, all of whom where also farmers. This is one of the key reasons why medieval battles tended to be fought in the springtime. If the farmers had not returned to the fields by the summer there would be no one to harvest the crops without which the manor would have starved through the winter.

Early Norman castles were built principally of wood as stone was expensive. Rothwell's location on the edge of a large wooded area and hunting park meant that there was no shortage of wood to be used for building. Wood was essential to a castle not just for building but also for repair. The life span of a timber castle was approximately 25 years before it rotted away.

A large number of people was needed to build a castle like the one at Rothwell, because it relied upon a man-made motte. This involved digging out the ditch, piling the soil in the middle and then compressing it. It is assumed William's Hill was a man-made motte, as the motte was abandoned in the mid-eleventh century in favour of a stone castle further down the hillside. The same appears to have been the case at Rothwell. The ditch ran between the Church and the castle site, along what is now Wood Lane. The motte appears to have been directly opposite the church, accessed by a bridge in later periods.

The Rothwell motte has now disappeared after mining waste was dumped on the site in the 18th and 19th centuries. In the 15th century the main manor house was constructed below the motte, but this incorporated a much older stone building.

Given that stone was expensive, this earlier building must have been of some importance. It is likely that this was an important domestic building. Stone buildings in the bailey indicate a permanent residential structure of post-1100s date. It was probably built in the bailey, because the motte was not strong enough to take the weight of the stone structure.

The stone remains of Rothwell castle indicate a construction date in the late 12th century; note the similarity between the remains at Rothwell and the Chapel walling at Middleham. It is likely that the stone remains in the bailey at Rothwell formed part of a substantial fortified manor house. It was certainly much more complicated than a simple shell keep, as this could have been built on top of a man-made motte, as demonstrated at Castle Acre, Norfolk, which gives us an idea of what Rothwell Castle may have looked like in its heyday.

Castle Acre was not a huge castle. Its small motte and shell keep show that most of the day-to-day life of the castle was conducted in the Bailey. The size and scale of Castle Acre appears to have been almost exactly the same as Rothwell. Built at the side of a small river crossing in the middle of pastures, the castle was used as a lordly retreat, the mediaeval equivalent of a house in the country.

The castle at Rothwell is recorded as the *Hospitium de Rowell* in the early 1200s. This does not mean a hospital but suggests a manor house where one would rest and relax. The medieval Latin reference sheds light upon Rothwell's importance. It was not a great defensive fortification like Middleham or Richmond but a place to rest (and enjoy hospitality) on a long journey or after an excursion in the hunting park. Castle Acre performed a similar function for the de Warenne family.

Castle Acre, because of its convenient location near the river crossing on the main route through the de Warenne estates, reflects Rothwell's castle in both its function and setting. The two castles are roughly contemporary, both being built in the aftermath of 1066 and in use well into the 13th century. Neither castle needed to be a huge fortification because of its proximity to a larger castle.

Rothwell's proximity to the main castle at Pontefract meant that it could only ever be a satellite, but it fulfilled an important role as administrative centre for the area in exactly the same way as Castle Acre did for the great castles of Norfolk, such as Castle Rising and Norwich Castle.

So, while Rothwell castle is now only a single stone pillar we can image how grand the site would have looked by comparing it to Castle Acre.

At Rothwell the great motte was abandoned but the site continued in use. Archaeological evidence has shown that the buildings in the bailey were retained and incorporated a splendid, stone built manor house, although by the mid 1400s this too was in need of tender loving care.

It is likely the 14th century manor house included a *solar* (a grand room for the lord), a Great Hall and ancillary buildings such as kitchens and storerooms.

The 14th century manor house, or certainly some of its out buildings, were incorporated into a house Roger Hopton built on the site in the 1480s. Roger Hopton's house was built in the then-popular half-timbered style. It is ironic to think that the original 'castle' 400 years earlier had stood on that site and nearly half a millennium later there was once again a timber structured building on the same site.

Not surprisingly, Hopton's manor was added to over the years and stood on the site until the late 20th Century when the building was demolished. That act consigned Rothwell's long history of manor houses and castles to the bookshelf leaving only memories for local people and little more than a footnote in our nation's history.

13th century manor house at Boothby Pagnell in Lincolnshire, which Rothwell's might have looked like.

Photographer unknown.

3. Why Kings of England Came To Rothwell

ONE OF THE REASONS FOR KINGS TO COME TO ROTHWELL would be to ensure that law and order was being maintained.

They might have delegated most of the administration of justice but occasionally the royal presence would be required.

We know there were several important lords (Thanes) in Rothwell and the surrounding villages during the time of the Anglo-Saxons who would report back to their Overlord, probably in the stronghold at Pontefract, and thence to the king.

When the Normans arrived with William the Conqueror they moved north taking lands from the Anglo-Saxons and dividing them among themselves as a reward for their loyalty to the King. Under William's guidance the lands were shared out relative to the degree of support they were perceived to have given.

Many Thanes resisted the change; they already had a fairly settled way of life with an advanced system of law and order and didn't want Norman rule or to be subservient to it.

William's answer to this was to lay waste the land between the rivers Humber and Tees – "The harrying of the North" – leaving the population homeless and destitute. Thanes who wouldn't change were taken from their lands and excecuted.

The peasants were also in revolt. Their only hope was to find shelter and sustenance in the forest.

In 1086, in the Doomsday Book, Rothwell was recorded as still having Anglo-Saxon Thanes whose land and holdings actually belonged to Ilbert de Lacy of Pontefract, or the king. At this time about 20% of the land in England belonged to the crown.

Ilbert de Lacy had been given the Honour of Pontefract by the king after the great service he had rendered at the Battle of Hastings and afterwards as the armies moved north. It didn't take long for de Lacy to start building a castle more suitable for a king than the hall used by the Anglo-Saxons which were usually made of wood.

Hunting was be an important part of life for the nobility, mainly for food but also for pleasure and sport. The Normans loved hunting and set aside large tracts of land just for this purpose, planting trees and shrubbery to encourage wildlife. There were several of these *heys* in this area most notably at Round Hey {Roundhay} and Rothwell Hey {Rothwell Haigh}, where a small castle or hunting lodge was built, large enough for a king and his retinue.

It is possible that it was built on a former Anglo-Saxon site, making use of the already productive fishponds and farmlands.

Hunting parks were quite well defined areas, often fenced and gated, and anyone found inside the park without authority would have suffered severe consequences.

What better reason for a king to go hunting than where there was game in plenty and suitable accommodation.

Thus, we have two reasons for kings to come to Rothwell; Law & Order and hunting.

Currently it is very difficult to date visits of kings to the area before King John, but we do know quite a lot about the de Lacy family based at Pontefract.

Rothwell was part of the Honour of Pontefract and contributed in many ways to the upkeep of the honour as a whole; tythes, servants and men required for fighting being examples. The de Lacies, it would appear, were quite close to the royal court and according to Batty, in his *History of Rothwell*, in 1189 Robert de Lacy was an attendant Baron at the coronation of Richard I.

When Robert died in 1192 without heirs, the estates passed to Albreda Lisours – a half sister – then to her grandson Roger Fitz Eustace, who assumed the surname of de Lacy.

During the reign of King John, Roger became the first sheriff of Yorkshire. Roger had a son, John, but died before the boy became of age. At this time minors such as John would have become a ward of the king and because he had been betrothed to a young girl, the daughter of the Earl of Shrewsbury, she too would have become a ward of the king. This meant that the two young people would have lived at the royal court until John became of age.

King John took advantage of this situation and visited Pontefract fairly often to keep an eye on things. He used the revenue from the Honour to fund other projects around the country.

He also loved hunting!

The park at Rothwell provided all he wished for – comfortable lodgings and plenty of sport. It is recorded that he stayed at Rothwell in 1212 – June 12th and September 8th/9th. He liked to travel the country with his judges and when official business was completed, what better way to

relax than a visit to Rothwell castle, which he called his "hospitium de Rowell."
When John de Lacy came of age he bought back the Honour of Pontefract from King John, who demanded 7000 marks when it was estimated that one hundred was a more appropriate sum.

Also, the king kept the castles at Pontefract and Darrington.

It was this kind of practice which caused the Barons to rise up against the king and John de Lacy was one of those who confronted him with the Magna Carta.

John de Lacy married well and, through his wife, inherited the title of Earl of Lincoln. He was one of those ordered by the king to bring the King of the Scots to York to meet Henry III.

History shows that monarchs travelled the country fairly frequently and after "work" needed to relax. Where better than one of the most prosperous honours such as Pontefract.

Edmund succeeded John de Lacy. He did much for the benefit of Rothwell. Even though it was a thriving community, he persuaded King John to grant the village the status of a market town and hold two fairs a year.

This is disputed by Albert Brown, who, quoting the Public Record Office, gives the date as 1408, being granted by Henry VII.

It is possible both are correct. Perhaps the earlier markets had been discontinued. Had the Black Death put an end to the gatherings and a new charter had had to be granted?

Edmund died in 1258 when his son, Henry, was only eight years old. Once again the king, Henry III (1216-1272) became guardian of the young boy and his estates and his bride-to-be, the daughter of the Earl of Salisbury. Consequently, Henry was brought up in the Royal household and would have become friends with the king's son, later Edward I.

When Henry de Lacy came of age he inherited the Honour of Pontefract and the title of Earl of Lincoln. He became a confidant of the king. Meanwhile Henry's mother was given 'a widow's dowry' which included the manor of Rothwell. Batty, in his History of Rothwell, states that she lived at the manor for about 40 years until her death.

Can one assume from this that, with the close connections and friendships with the Royal family, visits were made by Henry to his mother in the company of the king and took advantage of the sport of kings?

Edward II

John Lydgate produced this illustration of Edward II in 1431 some 104 years after his death. Edward II came to stay at Rothwell from 18th April to the beginning of May 1319. After a visit to York he returned to Rothwell on 3rd June leaving on the 8th June 1319. He came again to Rothwell where he stayed from the 15th May to 21st May 1323, only 4 years before his death in 1327.

Henry de Lacy had two sons, both of whom died accidentally in childhood. On his death in 1310 he bequeathed his estates to his daughter, Alice, who was married to Thomas Duke of Lancaster who now took control of Pontefract.

So, after 230 years, the de Lacy line came to an end.

As Thomas was the uncle of Edward II the castle at Pontefract was surely freely available to the king. It is thought that Edward came several times to Rothwell, mainly when the Scots were invading the north of England between 1314 and 1319.

The Scots were encamped at Rothwell, Batley and Morley and Edward issued writs from York and Pontefract to 'Gentlemen', who oversaw Wapentakes (areas of the kingdom covering several villages) to raise armies in order to fight the Scots. Between times he stayed at Rothwell as a base to fight or hunt – or both; he loved his sport.

According to Batty, he came again in May 1323 for several days and then went to Bishopthorpe, home of the Archbishop of York.

Not only was Edward having trouble with the Scots – they had been defeated at Bannockburn – the Knights of the Realm were also in conflict. The king's favourite, a Frenchman named Piers Gaveston, ridiculed them and Edward was so weak and besotted by him that he did not bring him to order.

The knights and nobles, led by Thomas of Lancaster, forced Edward to appoint some of their number to form a council – *Lords Ordinaires* – to oversee the government. But Edward was devious and didn't follow the rules.

At Scarborough Castle, Gaveston, the favourite, was captured and eventually executed. Not all the lords were in agreement and some supported the king, but Thomas of Lancaster stood firm and eventually it cost him his head.

Once again, Pontefract fell into the hands of the king.

When Edward III (1327-1377) married Phillipa he gave her parts of the Honour of Pontefract, which then passed to Henry, Earl of Lancaster, who died in 1360.

The monarchy seems to have had many connections with the area and once again we look to the sport of kings in the proximity of Rothwell.

In 1359 John of Gaunt, Earl of Richmond, and son of Edward III, married Blanche, daughter and heir of Henry, Earl of Lancaster. It is known that John of Gaunt spent the early months of his marriage at Rothwell and would want to survey his new acquisitions.

These covered a tremendous area from as far south as Warwick to Northumberland, and all of Yorkshire and Lancashire and part of Cheshire. Almost a country in itself!! These estates gave considerable wealth and power to John of Gaunt.

His visits to Rothwell are well noted, as well as his supposed killing of the last wild boar in the area.

Such is John o' Gaunt's significance, both nationally and locally, that he merits a chapter to himself.

On the death of Edward III in 1377 the political situation deteriorated.

The new king, Richard II, was only ten years old. His uncle, John o' Gaunt, who had already wielded considerable influence and power under Edward, assumed guardianship of the king's person and control over affairs of state.

Richard was no fighter. He preferred the good life. His clothes were very ostentatious and it is reported that he once spent 30,000 marks on a coat.

As the young king came of age and began to assert his own (albeit inadequate) authority, his relationship with his overbearing uncle became strained. Indeed, Richard came into conflict with many of the aristocracy, several of whom he banished from the kingdom.

One of these was John o'Gaunt's son, Henry Bolingbroke.

John o' Gaunt died in 1399.

Richard, no doubt relieved to be rid of his domineering uncle, sent soldiers to Rothwell Castle to strip it of its treasures and generally cause mayhem by breaking down fences and demolishing buildings, including the bridge to the church over what is now Wood Lane.

As it was Richard who ordered the destruction of Rothwell Castle and the looting of its treasures it is hardly likely that he would rebuild the property!

Only the keeper of Rothwell, John de Rothwell, was killed, but not before he had protested about the destruction of the property and the rough handling of his daughter, Lady Rose.

Soon after his father's death, Henry Bolingbroke returned to England to claim his inheritance.

Such was the support he received from disaffected nobles that he was encouraged to challenge the king who was in Ireland when Henry landed in the Humber estuary.

He swept through the North of England, captured the king on his return and imprisoned him in Pontefract castle.

During his incarceration a 'lady of the town' became his companion and Lady Rose was given the position of her supervisor – not an enviable job!

Henry deposed Richard and annexed the Duchy of Lancaster to the Crown of England.

When Richard died, under circumstances which have never been satisfactorily explained, Bolingbroke, styling himself Henry IV, was crowned on 13th October 1399 and ruled from 1399-1413.

This break in the line of descendants of Edward III laid the foundation for the Wars of the Roses during the following century.

Henry did not completely forget Rothwell though, and in 1408 he granted permission for a weekly market every Wednesday and two fairs every year.

Henry IV
From *Histoire du Ray d'Angleterre, Richard II* (French) *circa* 1401 – 1405 shows Parliament proclaiming Henry Bolingbroke Duke of Lancaster as King Henry VI of England in 1399 shortly after the death of John of Gaunt. Henry came to stay at Rothwell in the 15th century.

IT WOULD APPEAR THAT FROM THIS TIME ON, the castle deteriorated sadly. There is evidence that the area around the buildings was used by tenants but there is no mention of who lived in the house.

Perhaps after the death of John de Rothwell it remained empty.

The timber from the park was still being used to repair other buildings in the Honour of Pontefract, namely providing shingles for roofs, mill wheels and planking for the mill dams to shore up the stones.

In 1484 a Roger Hopton, Esq. appears on the scene, when, for 10s. he was granted the right of 'pannage of pigs' in the park. He lived at the manor of Ackworth.

In 1485, following the Battle of Bosworth Field which ended the Wars of the Roses, the victorious Henry Tudor (Henry VII) had a survey made of his Duchy of Lancaster.

Roger Hopton became tenant of the farm and manor on a 21-year lease, for which he was to pay a rental of £6 3s. 4d. *per annum.*

This was revised later when he was granted:

> *for 7 yrs from 29th September 1487 at £6. 16s. 8d. the site of the Manor of Acworth; the demesne lands and watermill, agistment of the park, hawking and the herbage and pannage of the park of Rothwell Haigh.*

In 1489/90 there is an entry referring to the:

> *farm of the garden of the Manor called Manor Garth with its appurtances in Rothwell let to Rog-*

> *er Hopton, esq. to have and to hold to him and his heirs and assigns forever by service according to the custom of the manor; Mr Hopton at his own expense to make in the Manor Garth a 'alairn' (hall) and parlour with a chamber and kitchen as appears by the court roll of this year'.*

He was clearly a gentleman of some substance (and, presumably, a faithful Lancastrian) for, by 1497, he had received a knighthood.

When Roger Hopton was given permission to build a more convenient and smaller house than the castle it was noted in the king's warrant of 27th August 1485 that, *the manor garth is in great 'ruyne' and decay*. It was also noted that, because of lack of maintenance it was almost falling down and there was no income to speak of apart from that brought in from the land tenants.

Because most of the fence around the park no longer existed, animals were roaming and now over ran the gardens and orchards!

* * * * * *

The carriage of the royal princesses
From the *Luttrell Psalter* (English) *circa* 1325 - 1335 and shows a golden coach which is carrying four crowned princesses. One can easily imagine such a coach carrying the king and queen of England to Rothwell.
©*British Library*

A report from

A progress made by the king's [Henry VII] council of his Duchy of Lancaster [1485] as followeth

Rothwell

Item

the park of Rothwell Haigh, whereof Roger Hopton is keeper, is great and large and the herbage thereof right hand <and> the great <part of the> [tree deleted] great and principal trees be felled down for the [kin deleted] reparation of the king's mills and other housings as he sayeth; and some be felled by the king's warrants under his signet, and <some by> the warrants of my lord of Gloucester and Sir James Haryngton as steward, which warrants he hath showed to the king's council.

Item

the manor of Rothwell is feebly repaired, specially the chapel, the hall, the chambers betwist the hall and the chapel chamber, which hall and chambers so un-repaired is thought to be taken down, and that the said chapel and chambers next adjoining thereunto should be repaired and kept up.

Item

<it is thought good> that the chamber of timber standing next the [far deleted] west end of the said chapel and the chamber standing at the

lower end of the said hall, and also the old kitchen adjoining to them, should be taken down, and the timber thereof laid up dry until the time the king's good grace be communed with, to understand whether his grace will that a new hall with other necessary houses of office be made there with the same timber or not.

John of Gaunt who came to stay at Rothwell on a number of occasions in the 14th century.

4. John of Gaunt

JOHN O' GAUNT WAS A VERY POWERFUL MAN in England in the mid-14th Century. He was the fourth son of the much loved and respected Edward III and his queen, Philippa of Hainault.

Their eldest child, Prince Edward, was invested by his father as the first Prince of Wales, but he was better known throughout his life, as The Black Prince. He married Joan of Kent. In 1376, when their son Richard was only 9 years old, he died.

The boy was only ten when he succeeded to the throne when Edward III died in the following year.

His uncle, John o' Gaunt, became his mentor and guardian and helped Richard to rule to such an extent that many people thought that he was aiming to become king himself. During the last years of Edward's reign John had helped him to rule, and when Richard became king, John just continued as before.

John was born in 1340 in Ghent, in Flanders, now called Belgium, and it is a corruption of 'Ghent' that gave him his famous sobriquet 'Gaunt' He was born when his mother accompanied his father on one of his forays into Flanders, in an effort to gain more land. Little is known of his early life, but he was created Earl of Richmond in 1342 and it is thought that he may have spent some of his youth in the household of his elder brother Edward, the Black Prince.

To understand how John became involved in the Rothwell area, it is necessary to go back some 250 years, to the time following the Norman invasion of England by William the Conqueror. Great swathes of land were given to his barons, as a reward for their loyalty, and a large area around Pontefract was given to one Ilbert de Lacy. His descendent Henry de Lacy had a daughter, Alice (he had had 2 sons, but both had died accidentally while still young) and when it came time for her to marry, the chosen groom was Thomas, Earl of Lancaster. Thomas was a cousin of King Edward II, Edward III's father. The land owned by the Earl was rich and included well-stocked hunting parks, forests and properties.

The properties of the de Lacy family were inherited by Alice on the death of her father, Henry, in 1310, and so by her husband, the Earl of Lancaster.

With so much land across Lancashire and Yorkshire, Thomas now felt powerful enough to challenge the King and fought for the throne at the battle of Boroughbridge, in 1322, but he was defeated, and was brought back to Pontefract Castle. He was tried for treason, and later executed, and the King reclaimed his land.

Edward III restored it to Henry de Lacy, when the Duchy of Lancaster was created in 1351. On 19th May 1359, in Reading Abbey, John o' Gaunt married Blanche, Henry's daughter, and they spent their early married life in the Manor House at Rothwell, which had become a favourite of the family, since the time of Alice's marriage to Thomas.

In 1361 Blanche's father, Henry, died and the title passed through her to John, making him the richest and most powerful man in the country.

There are many references to the fact that Rothwell Manor was a particularly favourite residence of John's. J

Batty writes *"Here lived the great John of Gaunt, and had a bridge of stone over the deep cut way, that is, betwixt the Church and the Manor House, whereby his family might pass to the church"*. This was in the area that is now Wood Lane.

John was, apparently, not always as faithful to Blanche as he might have been. Blanche gave him three children, the first of whom was Henry Bolingbroke, so called because he was born in Bolingbroke Castle in Lincolnshire. He later became Henry IV. The nanny employed to look after them, Catherine Swynford, was believed to have been John's mistress for many years, and she did in fact become his 3rd wife in 1395. The story also goes that John fought one of his stewards, John of Rothwell, over a certain serving wench, and as John o' Gaunt was a very tall and well built man there is little doubt as to who won the fight. The event is said to have taken place in the churchyard on a moonlit night and the remains of poor John of Rothwell were buried under a yew tree near the west door of the church.

There is yet another story about his exploits whilst staying in Rothwell. J Batty says,

> *"It is reported that on one of his hunting expeditions in this quarter, he killed the last wild boar frequenting these parts; so the legend runs. And the probability of the affair is strengthened by the fact, that the spot where it is said to have taken place, is called "Stye-Bank" to this day; and, being a wild common even down to about eighty-nine years ago, was a very likely little nook for such animals to exist in. No doubt the event would*

cause great consternation in the neighbourhood, for it would be a terror to the inhabitants, and they would look upon this said John of Gaunt as a kind of deliverer from its annoyance".

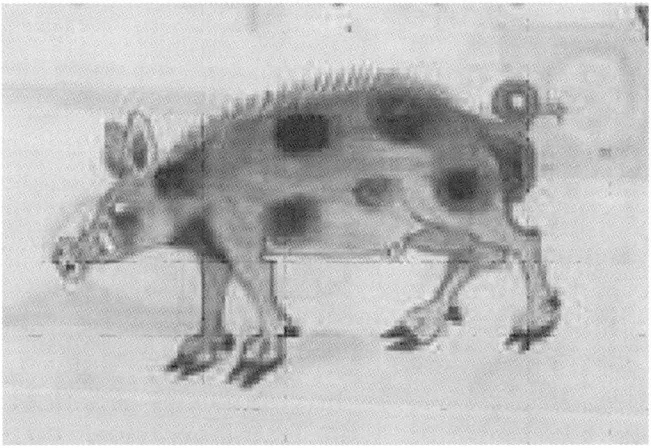

An illustration from the *Luttrell Psalter* (English) *circa* 1325 - 1335 showing a wild boar. The Normans would have valued the hunting of this creature as it was not uncommon for them to defend themselves fiercely and would have taken some skill to hunt. According to local folklore John o' Gaunt killed the last wild boar in Rothwell, but there appears to be no documentary evidence to substantiate this legend.
©British Library

This is a charming tale, but another source of it says that John o'Gaunt killed the last wild WOLF in England, so it seems the truth of it will always remain a mystery.

Blanche was a very beautiful young woman, and the poet Geoffrey Chaucer wrote a very famous poem about her called *"The Deth of Blaunche the Duchesse"*, in which John o' Gaunt features as a 'sylvan knight'. The fact that

John was reputed to be almost 7 feet tall, and was very broad, seems to have escaped his notice. Chaucer was married to Catherine Swynford's younger sister, and was often in the company of John, so he obviously used a great deal of poetic licence on this occasion. This poem was written as a memorial to Blanche in 1369, soon after her death, of the plague, at the age of 29.

Despite the death of his wife John was often in the North of England, and was always ready to defend England if the Scots should invade. In 1371 he married Constance of Castile, and continued to support his father Edward III in affairs of state, as well as going off to wars in France and Spain.

A detailed account of the life and times of John o' Gaunt has been written by Anthony Goodman, and according to this work John and his entourage spent the first two weeks of September, 1374 in Yorkshire, "visiting his castle at Pontefract, and his hunting lodge in Rothwell".

Edward III died in 1377 and Richard, his grandson, became king but his uncle, John, still continued to run the country as before, but by 1385 they had differences of opinion about political matters. Richard II was still young, and inexperienced, and had very little knowledge of military affairs so they often quarrelled, but still John's main object was to run the country as he had done for a long while. He often stayed in the North of England, and according to Anthony Goodman "in the latter part of September that year Gaunt was at Lancaster and other places in Lancashire: on 5 October, just over a fortnight before the opening of Parliament, he was at his hunting lodge at Rothwell (Yorks.)" He also notes that ducal warrants were issued in Lancs. and Rothwell in September 1385.

Towards the middle of the 1390's his second wife died, and in 1396 he finally married his long-time mistress, Catherine Swynford, much to everyone's amazement. According to Anthony Goodman "He was probably with her at Pontefract Castle on 23 February and 10 March and at Rothwell soon afterwards. Perhaps they were touring his estates so that Catherine might first be received as a duchess by his provincial retainers and tenants, likely to be more gracious to her than censorious kinsfolk, backbiting royal courtiers and rude Londoners."

There are many stories about John o Gaunt and some say that he was the author of some of the early ballads about 'Robin Hood'. I'm sure that this would be hotly disputed by the good folk of Nottingham, but there *is* an area just outside Rothwell with that very name, after all! The one thing that is, however, very unlikely to be 'just a story' is that fact, which is well documented, that despite being the Duke of Lancaster he only spent 9 days in the town of Lancaster itself.

John o' Gaunt died in 1399 but his association with the hunting lodge at Rothwell did not really end with his death.

John's son Henry had upset both Edward III and Richard II and had been banished to France for 10 years, but soon after his father died Henry came back to England. Richard II was, conveniently, in Ireland and Henry landed on the East Coast. He swept through the North of England, deposed Richard II and annexed The Duchy of Lancaster to the Crown of England. His coronation took place on 13th. October 1399 and this split in the descendants of Edward III laid a foundation for the Wars of the Roses during the following century. Henry did not completely forget Rothwell, though, and in 1408 he granted a Wednesday Market, weekly, and two Fairs every year.

At the time of writing *"History of Rothwell"*, in 1877, Batty writes,

> *"before leaving this interesting building, it may be stated that there is a pewter tankard which has been preserved for many generations in the house, out of which it is affirmed that the noted John of Gaunt drank. When in perfect condition it would hold about two quarts. It has a lid with hinge attached, which can be lifted by the thumb. It is after the pattern of those silver pitchers used for warm spiced ale, and handed round at funerals. There used to be a set of round pewter plates and dishes to match".*

The house referred to here is the timber-framed house, still to be seen in Rothwell, built by Roger Hopton at the request of King Henry VII. After the Manor House fell into disrepair He wanted a smaller property when he came to visit Rothwell, although even this house eventually became, derelict, and had to be rebuilt in the form it is today.

There is one more relic in Rothwell to remind us of John o' Gaunt. In the vestry of Rothwell Church is a coat or jacket that is said to have been worn by John. It is sleeveless, and measures some 19 inches across the back, which is very large, particularly as most people at that time were small of stature It was made of strong canvas and padded with sheep's wool and was in three layers.

According to Batty,

> *"some fifty or sixty years ago there were some pieces of armour and a helmet, these were sent to the Tower of London, by one of the vicars. The late John Smith remembered that these relics were kept in the vestry chamber, seventy-five years ago, and approached by ladder. The coat he saw was cloth-faced, and had steel ribs at half inch intervals. It is only right to state that several gentlemen of antiquarian repute have thrown discredit upon this coat's connection with John of Gaunt, and they deem it merely an ordinary jacket of a common soldier of the period".*

It seems, then, that this may be just another "John o' Gaunt" story, but at least this one seems to have a little more substance than many of the others.

5. Medieval Hunting

TODAY HUNTING IS ASSOCIATED more with the middle and upper classes in society and the local hunts which are held, those at Bodsworth, York and Ainsty serve more as social occasions. The sight of the modern hunt turning out was very spectacular and colourful until it was made illegal.

However in medieval times this was very different and whereas the modern hunt is sport, in medieval times it had other purposes including the provision of food and to assist the arable land owners to rid themselves of vermin and other beasts which would, if not controlled, devour the crops before they could be harvested.

The fox has always been a predator, seizing lambs in the springtime and ducks, hens, geese and the like are killed by them irrespective of the need for food.

The greatest medieval impetus for hunting was the need for fresh meat.

Because of the cost of feeding animals throughout the winter period, animals (cattle, sheep etc.) would be slaughtered and the meat preserved in salt which, as the months progressed would begin to taste foul. Therefore the chance of freshly killed meat would be an attraction to gentry and peasant alike.

In medieval times the right to hunt was only allowed to the privileged and indeed in 1390 Richard II issued a Statute of the Realm which decreed that only persons with lands and tenements to the value of 40 shillings per year would be allowed to hunt with snares, hounds or ferrets and so stopped the commoner from undertaking such practices.

The main quarry for the huntsman would be deer, which in most hunting areas of medieval times would, in the main, be quite plentiful. Venison would be the feast of local lord of the manor and his invited friends.

The great hart itself was a majestic beast with an age of six years and possessing antlers of ten tines. The antlers, together with their light frame made them both a dangerous and cunning prey to contest.

Hunting wild hart in medieval times was conducted by royal consent. During the Middle Ages they were hunted to such an extent that numbers throughout Europe fell dramatically.

To preserve stocks in forests and parks they were maintained by buck stalls which consisted of a woodland enclosure surrounded by a shallow fence which in turn was surrounded by a ditch of some depth – known as a deer leap. This would prevent the beast escaping.

A royal hunt

This French image if from the *Smithfield Decretals* by Raymund of Penafort, *fl.* 1300 - 1340, showing a monarch hunting a stag with his dog.

In the priority stakes the wild boar was a poor second and these again were very dangerous animals to hunt with their sharp protruding tusks and undoubted use of their strength.

The King Hunting

From the *Queen Mary Psalter* (English) *circa* 1310 – 1320 and showing a royal hunting scene. The king on horse back is blowing a horn with two mounted companions preceded by a youth with two dogs. It is likely that this is Edward II (1307 – 1327) and could quite easily be of him hunting at Rothwell.

Wild boar existed in England during the Middle Ages and it is reputed that John of Gaunt slew the last wild boar in England in our own Rothwell in 1398, although some accounts dispute this and claim a wild wolf as the more likely victim.

Forest and woodland was certainly the terrain in which wild boar would exist and a 15th Century book of hunting gives specific details for the slaying and hunting of Wild Boar.

The hare would be another attractive, but somewhat cunning, quarry and the killing of these would provide good meat with the added advantage that its death would stop it destroying crops. That too would be so in the case of the rabbit.

The main weapon of the hunt was the longbow which a skilful handler could fire to a distance of up to three hundred paces with accuracy. The use of the bow in medieval times was learnt from an early age as the law demanded that all males should become proficient so that at any time any man could be conscripted for military service.

The arrows which were used were of the barbed type and these would be used in the hunting of the deer and the wild boar or wolf. When they struck the target they would not fall out as the animal tried to escape.

In later years the crossbow came into use and the bolt could be used over a greater distance with supreme accuracy. These in turn could be of the barbed variety.

The spear would be used at close quarters and in some instances the javelin could be hand thrown with great accuracy and at a long distance.

The skilled hunter would, in some cases, use the hunting sword when tackling large game, particularly at the time of the final kill. Most of the huntsmen would carry a hunting knife which could be used for cutting up the carcase of a dead deer or wild boar.

A rabbit warren

From the *Queen Mary Psalter* (English) *circa* 1310 – 1320 and shows two rabbits facing each other on top of the mound while a hunting animal enters the central burrow. Other rabbits run in and out of other burrows. Rabbits would have been classed as minor animals of the chase and were part of the peasant's table.

More common of course would be a snare used for trapping and killing of rabbit and hare. This would be the main 'hunting weapon' of the peasant in his illegal poaching for his meat. Stray deer, or even wolf, could be caught this way, if the trap was appropriately placed.

Other quarry to be hunted were the badger, and for this purpose the three-pronged otter spear would be used.

The weapons used by the upper classes would often be family treasures, passed from generation to generation.

Of course each Lord of the Manor would have his pack of hounds which would be given the scent of the hart or deer.

The deer itself, when being chased, could double back on itself, hopefully throwing the hounds into confusion. After a long chase the hart may plunge itself into water to throw off the scent and also to cool its sweaty, heated body. When this happened the Master of the Hunt would recognise this was a sign that the hart was ready to yield, either to the hounds in the water or to be taken on the bank.

The correct approach for the kill was for the master or one of the nobles to move in behind the beast and sever a muscle in one of the hind legs. The final kill was achieved by the application of a sword between the neck and the antlers to sever the spinal cord. In some cases however it was more suitable to achieve the final kill by using a bow.

From what is gathered from ancient manuscripts and what is said of modern hunting that death was quick.

At the time of death the hounds would be allowed to bite at the flesh and lap the blood. This would be part of their training, especially any younger or more inexperienced of their number, to improve their keenness on future occasions.

After this, the next step would be to split the carcass, or as is known in hunting terms, 'breaking up the beast'. This would involve slitting the beast down the belly, stripping the hide, removing the hind quarters and the loins.

Forest laws in medieval times specified hunting seasons for beasts and animals although in statute law there was no legislation for this . However the following seasons were observed:

Red Deer Stag:	*June 14th to September 14th*
Red Deer Hind:	*September 14th to January 6th*
Fallow Deer Buck:	*June 14th to September 14th*

Fallow Deer Doe:	*September 14th to February 8th*
Roe Deer Buck:	*Easter to September 29th*
Roe Doe:	*September 29th to February 2nd*
Hare:	*September 29th to February 2nd or June 24th*
Wild Boar:	*September 14th, 29th or Christ mas Day to February 2nd*
Wolf:	*Christmas to March 25th but probably all year*
Fox:	*September 8th or Christmas Day to March 25th*
Otter:	*February 22nd to June 24th*

Marten, Badger and Rabbit could be hunted in all seasons.

These dates were compiled to give dignity to the hunted beast. In medieval times, when the hunter was looked upon as a 'noble', this would be honoured as a gesture of fairness to the hunted quarry. It would also allow the animals to breed and thus preserve stocks of game. The hunter of the day, being usually of the well educated type, would realise that, if these rules were not adhered to, numbers could very quickly be exhausted.

The art of horse breeding was established in the Arab countries where many war horses were bred. It was only in the Middle Ages however that specialised breeding of horses for specific purposes began to be established in Europe.

As part of their education sons of the gentry would have to learn, not only the skills of riding, javelin throwing and archery, but also what to look for in purchasing a good horse suitable for the needs of war and hunting.

For the hunt a man would dress in attire which, while looking smart, would not hinder his movement. Narrow sleeves, a tunic (which would not come below the knee) and boots were the order of the day. Some documents say colour was not important but that common sense would prevail. Indeed in the case of the lone hunter or outlaw, for whom camouflage would be an asset, green would become the prominent colour.

These colours were adopted by professional hunt servers and Yeoman of the Forest. From childhood times we have always pictured Robin Hood and his Merry Men clad in Lincoln Green.

Fishing was another aspect of medieval hunting. Although it did not involve the thrill of the kill and chase it provided a cheap sport. It was regarded as a tame pursuit but required skill both in the 'angling' method and in the use of the fly in pursuit of game fish – Salmon, Trout etc. Eels were plentiful in mill ponds and provided a cheap alternative on the table.

Some peasants were very skilful in the use of the sling which, by projecting a stone, could, in some cases, kill a deer. They were loath to use the longbow as they could easily be detected and face the drastic consequences.

The dogs used in hunting in medieval times would usually be the greyhound or the retriever. These were usually kept in kennels and would be brought to where the Master of the Hunt required them. They would respond to the sound of the hunting horn.

What of hunting in Rothwell around this time?

It is common knowledge that when the Normans conquered Britain the first thing William did was to reward his barons for their assistance in his victory. He gave this part of the country to Ilbert De Lacy who set up his headquarters in a grand and magnificent castle at Pontefract.

Indeed, the area he commanded stretched from Pontefract to Blackburn in Lancashire. It was known as the Honour of Pontefract.

The area around Rothwell was covered by a large forest some two miles long and one mile wide. It was also covered in lush grass and vegetation. It afforded prime hunting land being well populated with deer, hart, wild boar, wolf, rabbits and hares.

Man with hunting dogs
From the *Luttrell Psalter* (English) *circa* 1325 - 1335 showing a man ready to unleash a couple of hunting dogs - a common scene in 14th century Rothwell.

It came as no surprise that it was reserved to create a hunting park or 'hay'. Another such area was created to the north of Leeds, known as Roundhay. To keep the animals in, and to keep the unwanted out, the area was surrounded by a palisade fence of hawthorn on a mound. To house the guests who would be taking part in the hunting and other sports it was decided to build a residence, locally called Rothwell Castle.

This appeared in 1087 and eventually became the administration centre for the honour of Pontefract. Ilbert De Lacy and his descendants would hold hunting parties, probably on a regular basis, and we know that King John visited Rothwell in 1212 in order to attend the hunting.

The park would be rich in game, as previously mentioned. The park had gates and we have Lofthouse Gate, Thwaite Gate and Lingwell Gate which could have been the entries to the the park.

At the end of the hunt there would be a great banquet, with food, wine and merriment. It is known the site had its own brewhouse, thus ale would be plentiful.

It is thought the hounds were kept in kennels on Rothwell Haigh and locally we have the South Leeds suburb of Hunslet, or 'Hounds Let', as the history books tell us how the name was derived.

Hunting would no doubt be on horseback with the hunters using longbows, crossbows, javelins and spears etc.

By the 14th century the site had come into the ownership of the Duchy of Lancaster and the hunting was taken over by the great John of Gaunt. Indeed it is generally accepted that John of Gaunt in 1398 slew the last wild boar in the Styebank Lane area of Rothwell. It is possible 'Styebank' got its name as the area where wild boar bred.

To the west of the area, Rothwell Castle also had its fish ponds where eels and other fish would be caught, providing sport and, of course in medieval times, fresh meat for the table.

Rothwell should be proud of its Royal connections in the hunting field.

King John hunting
A 14th century illustration of King John hunting a stag with hounds. A sight that may have been familiar while he was hunting at Rothwell.

6. Medicine

THE MIDDLE AGES WAS NOT A GOOD TIME to be ill. Doctors were few and far between, and such remedies as they used were not usually scientific, and were very rarely effective.

Rothwell would have had the same provision for medical care as any village in the North of England, that is: experienced older women, who were able to cope with most minor ailments, an apothecary, and, if necessary, Nostell Priory might have been asked for assistance.

There would most likely have been a physician at the manor house when the nobility was in residence, but they would not have been available to the local people who could not afford to pay. In any case, peasants were expendable, and there were plenty more where they came from!

Most doctors worked on the basis of prevention rather than cure and often advised a special diet in the hope of preventing an ailment from becoming more serious. For instance moist foods like chicken and milky dishes were felt useful to cool the body down.

The four 'humours', Earth, Air, Fire and Water, had to be in the correct proportions for the body to remain healthy. When they became unbalanced action had to be taken.

Even in those times it was acknowledged that a healthy diet, exercise and lack of stress were essential elements in the well being of all their patients. Exercise was fairly easy to maintain, with the amount of physical work that had to be done in all walks of life, but the diet and lack of stress were not so easily achievable.

One of the methods for diagnosing illness was to carefully examine the urine of the patient, collected in a chamber pot. The colour determined what the illness was and what was the best way to cure it, and subsequently it would tell the doctor if, and when, the patient was recovering. Some doctors made a diagnosis by examining blood or faeces of the patient, and others took the patients pulse.

With the diagnosis made, the doctor then had to decide on the treatment. The most usual remedy was to give the patient an enema, but other treatments played their part. Laxatives, mostly in the form of herbal remedies, were prescribed, and the herbs had to be picked at a certain time, from a particular place and sometimes even by a certain type of person, such as a young maiden, or a child, for the remedy to be effective.

Another laxative used very frequently was rhubarb, and, while there is no guarantee that it was growing around Rothwell at that time, it would seem a distinct possibility, in view of it's proliferation in the more recent past.

For some only a hot bath was required; an herbal diuretic would do the trick for others, but it was all very hit and miss.

Bloodletting was often used and it depended on the illness as to what part of the body was cut to allow the blood to flow. Great care had to be taken to ensure that the cut was not too deep and sometimes this 'cure' had disastrous results, leading to the death of the patient.

There is little doubt that Rothwell would have had its fair share of ladies blessed with healing hands, and these women often used herbs for curing toothache, boils and other minor illnesses. Where they really came into their own, though, was helping women with problems associated with childbirth. Their help was often sought for menstrual problems, conception, pregnancy and the birth itself. When herbs failed these 'wise women' would resort to the magic arts.

It is not really surprising that so many mothers died in childbirth and that the infant mortality rate was very high.

Surgery was always looked upon as a last resort, but sometimes it was considered necessary. The only substances available to kill pain were likely to kill the patient too. Various analgesics were concocted from hemlock and opium but they had to be applied in the exact amounts. Often too little would be given, to be on the safe side, and the patient would have been in dreadful pain throughout the whole operation.

The original surgeons were the butchers. In fairness, they did their best. The one fear the surgeons had was that in plying their trade, for a fee, they would accidentally kill someone and be charged with murder!

During the Middle Ages apothecaries became more common and they produced a 'cure all' remedy they called 'theriac', which was commonly known as treacle. It was used to cure everything from fevers to diabetes and from skin blemishes to broken limbs, but whether it actually did cure everything is open to question.

'Treacle' was made in England under licence, but it had originally come from the Middle East, where the Arabs had formulated it, before the knowledge came to the West. It took many years to be made and even longer to mature, and inevitably some people tried to make inferior versions, which were cheaper, but whether they were any less efficacious is still unknown.

A healthy life in the middle ages was very much down to genes and being in the right place at the right time, and, whilst being rich and having access to a doctor might help, it often made things worse. Maybe the peasants weren't so badly off after all.

7. The Plague

DURING THE 1330S AND THE EARLY PART OF THE 1340s Rothwell was a prosperous, lively village where everyone went about their business, blissfully unaware of the disaster which was about to befall them.

The Black Death had arrived in Italy in 1348 and it was gradually making its way westwards and northwards until, in 1349, disaster struck. The plague arrived in England in just one port - Melcombe Regis, near Weymouth, in Dorset. From there it spread throughout the whole of the country.

The Midlands were the worst hit, but there was no stopping it, once it took hold.

It is hard to imagine how the people of Rothwell would have felt when their once prosperous village was hit by this tragedy. The smell of death pervaded the atmosphere, along with the smell of vegetables rotting in the fields and animals dying from hunger.

The plague was no respecter of age or status; rich and poor alike were struck down suddenly, sometimes in the street, or in their own homes. Neighbours became suspicious of neighbours, and even families refused to visit each other, for fear of becoming infected.

Sometimes parents died, leaving children to fend for themselves as best they could. There was no one to tend to the animals or to harvest the crops and, for those not taken, it became a battle of wits to stay alive.

If they went out to scavenge for food a passing stranger might infect them, but if they stayed in the village they would very likely starve. What a choice!

Vinegar was one source of hope to which people clung. It added to the strange mixture of smells in the air around the village, but it was the only readily available means known to be effective against the infection, although the reason why it was effective was not yet understood.

Many villages installed "plague stone" which were in fact large bowls, made of stone. They were placed on the road into the village, and filled with vinegar. Money was put into them so that any traders, or possibly monks, could leave provisions and in return would be able to take payment without fear of catching the plague from the disinfected coins.

It is said a surviving plague stone from the Rothwell area stood in the entrance lobby of Methley Primary School for many years.

Carts came round at night to collect the dead, and there were too many bodies for the local cemetery, so pits were dug, and all the dead were thrown into the pit together, and covered in lime, and then a thin layer of earth, and left to rot. There is believed to be an example of a burial pit in the Rothwell area, at Robin Hood.

There were three types of plague, which devastated the world in the early 14th Century. The first two, the septicaemic – which attacked the blood, and the pneumonic - which affected the lungs, were always fatal.

The third type of plague was the Bubonic, originated in China, which was one of the busiest trading nations in the world at that time. The many ships that came into the ports to trade were invaded by rats that carried the plague in their blood stream. The rats, in turn, were infested with fleas, which bit the rats and carried the disease to the humans.

This disease was very infectious. It quickly spread among the crew and by the time the ships docked in European ports many of them were already dead.

Some Friars and Nuns came to care for the sick, but they too became ill and carried it back into the cities. Thus the dreadful years began. There was no one to care for the sick or bury the dead and death was everywhere.

Once the disease struck it could kill with terrifying speed. The Italian writer, Boccaccio, said its victims often

> *"Ate lunch with their friends and dinner with their ancestors in Paradise".*

Gradually the plague spread north and eventually reached England, where it was called 'The Black Death' because of the colour of the spots on the body. It began with a fever and swelling in the lymph glands. These were called 'buboes', which is why it is called "bubonic" plague, and they were very painful. When the spots appeared they were red, but they quickly turned black and when that happened there was little hope of survival, and whole villages were wiped out at a stroke.

People tried all kinds of things in an effort to ward of the disease They carried herbs, such as lemon, camphor and pine and they soaked their handkerchiefs in various aromatic oils to try to avoid catching the dreaded plague.

Another way they tried to stop the disease coming to a particular village was to loudly ring the bells in the church in the hope that their religious fervour would find favour with God.

There was some respite during the winter months because the carrier fleas were dormant at that time, but in the spring the whole process began again.

In 1348 the Pope sent a message to a group of notable doctors in Paris and asked them to look into the causes of this awful disease, which was wiping out so much of the population in the whole of Europe.

They didn't really come up with any answers, but they made some very strange recommendations, such as:

Do not eat meat, fish or poultry
Do not eat olive oil, as it is poisonous
Do not cook in rainwater
Do not bathe or sleep in the daytime, as both are dangerous

Other doctors advised people not to think about death but to think happy thoughts and to visit fine gardens, especially when the flowers are in bloom, or to listen to nice music to take their mind off what could happen. It was also suggested that they might like to look at gold, silver or any other precious metals or pretty coloured stones, although where the common people were likely to find these precious jewels was not even hinted at.

Nothing seemed to stop the plague from spreading and a group of men felt it their duty to atone for the sins of the people which had brought this awful disaster upon them. They were called 'Flagellants' and they went through the streets doing penance by thrashing themselves with homemade whips. These were made of hard, knotted leather and they had spikes attached, which drew blood at every stroke. Their idea was that if they suffered, like Jesus, God would forgive the people and take away the plague, but sadly it had no effect at all.

In 1349 The Pope banned the organisation, and ordered all authorities to suppress them, but they constantly re-appeared whenever the plague reared it's ugly head, well into the 15th Century.

The plague affected everyone, rich and poor alike. The noted Florentine Historian Villani wrote, *"and many lands and cities were made desolate. And the plague lasted until ...."*.

Villani left a blank space at the end of the sentence, intending to fill it in later, after the plague had ended.

He never did. He died of the plague in 1348.

The pattern continued for about five years and, even when the worst was, over people lived in fear of the sporadic outbreaks which continued right up to 1665 when the Great Plague wiped out so many people in London.

In the five years from 1347 to 1352 it is estimated that 25 million people in Europe died of the plague, which was approximately one third of the total population.

The results of this devastating plague were far-reaching. So many peasants had died that the labour force was very much reduced and those who were left were under so much pressure of work that they felt emboldened to ask for more wages.

This request was refused, but a few privileges were granted. As time went on memories began to fade and the peasants felt that these rights might be taken away and they would be back to square one. It was the growth of a string of 'workers' rights' issues that eventually led to The Peasants' Revolt in 1381.

The fact that Rothwell had been so prosperous before the plague meant that it was able to survive, but it was probably a very different village from what it had been before the plague.

All over the country villages were desperate to farm the land as before, but there was just not enough skilled labour. The peasants realised that this gave them power to ask for more money.

The nobility felt that the peasants could do very little to further their cause. To add to the problem, more money than ever was needed in the way of taxes.

This was because the King at that time, Richard II, was only a minor. His Uncle John o' Gaunt was running the country on His behalf. The economic state of the country was not foremost in his mind. He was more interested in fighting in France and Spain, so he ordered a Poll Tax of 4d. or 5d. per acre, per year to be imposed on all people aged 14 and over.

The story goes that a tax inspector called upon a certain house in Dartford, Kent, and demanded Poll Tax for the daughter of the house. The mother protested that the girl was not of age. The tax inspector in turn insisted that she *was* old enough, and proceeded to convince them by raping her on the spot.

The girl's father, Wat Tyler, was so incensed that he gathered other malcontents together and marched on London.

In Essex too there was trouble with a tax collector. Such was the mood in the countryside that word quickly spread and the peasants mobilised. By the time they reached London the two 'armies' had merged. They burnt all tax documents that came into their hands on the way!

King Richard was only 14 at the time, but he promised to consider their demands and asked them to go home.

Some did, but others carried on and captured the Tower of London, killing the Archbishop of Canterbury and the Treasurer on the way.

The young king bravely faced the peasants' army at Smithfield to negotiate. The atmosphere of the meeting was tense. When Wat Tyler clutched Richard's arm and called him "brother" members of the king's entourage reacted and cut him down.

The peasants dispersed after that, but none of the promises was kept and things gradually drifted back into the old ways.

It took another 100 years or so for the peasants to gradually realise their worth. Eventually there were so few of them left to work the fields that they could threaten to withdraw their labour, and the lord of the manor had no choice but to pay them their due.

The plague itself was very unpleasant, to put it mildly, but at least it was responsible for some small improvement in the lives of the common people.

There were other repercussions too.

During the years the plague was rampant the peasants and noblemen alike were in churches everywhere praying for deliverance from this scourge. When no deliverance came it caused people to question why God had let this happen and many people lost their faith.

Even the world of art was affected. Many churches and city councils commissioned copies of 'Danse Macabre – Dance of Death' to hang in their buildings to commemorate this great event in everyone's life. These pictures depicted skeletons dancing in the street with the living, young girls dancing with death, and even babies being snatched from their mothers arms. The word 'macabre' was certainly appropriate, and reminded both rich and poor of their mortality.

The plague also had an unexpected effect on the language used in England. When William first conquered England bringing his noblemen with him, the official language in England became French, although the peasants still continued to use the indigenous Anglo-Saxon, with its various dialects. But during the years of the Black Death so many French speakers and teachers of the language had been wiped out, that the French Language gradually disappeared and, by l362, English was once again the official Language.

Thank goodness that the rich Yorkshire dialect of the people of Rothwell and the surrounding area was not lost forever.

8. Health

THE HEALTH OF PEOPLE IN THE ROTHWELL area was very likely to be similar to that of most people in the rest of England.

Life expectancy in the Middle Ages was very different from today. Very few people lived until the age of 70 but the majority died much younger, indeed half of all babies born died before they were five years old.

There were many reasons for this: plagues, famine, wars and a general bad diet. Even childbirth itself was a much riskier business at that time.

The average life expectancy for a man was about 28 years and possibly a little longer for a woman. Even monks, in their closed environment were not immune. Monks were not bound by the rules of chastity that later applied, and their average age at death was a measly 30 years.

Leprosy was another very serious disease and was responsible for many deaths. It was incorrectly assumed to be sexually transmitted. Lepers were outcasts, not so much for their illness but because they were lumped together with heretics, Jews and homosexuals, so they were avoided for the wrong reasons, but with the best results in the end.

Illnesses were thought to be a punishment from God for sins committed. For example, if someone became afflicted with madness it was assumed that it was because he had been a glutton or maybe a sexual deviant.

Lunacy was also thought to have been brought on by demons or even by the position of the planets, and the term itself, 'lunacy', derives from the Latin for 'moon'.

At the other end of the scale, it was believed that laziness cooled the blood, and turned to listlessness and melancholy.

The majority of people lived very closely together and even the odd pig was sometimes housed in the same dwelling as a large family, so it was hardly surprising that disease, once it had taken hold, spread very rapidly.

Toilet arrangements were very basic; just a box over a hole in the ground. In the manor houses the toilet, or *garderobe* as it was known, would be in an upstairs room, with plenty of space below. The fumes that seeped into the room did an excellent job in keeping the moths at bay.

The ordinary peasant's house was not so well served. Any fumes had to escape through open doors and windows or, in the winter, camouflaged by the smoke from the fire curling up from the centre of the room and out of the hole in the roof.

Rats also spread diseases. We have seen in the previous chapter how they were the carriers of plague.

With so many ailments about it is obvious that many people would die before anything could be done for them. Doctors, midwives, nuns, apothecaries and even housewives did their best to treat the sick, but they fought a losing battle and many who survived, but were too ill to work, had no option but to resort to begging.

Many remedies were tried in an effort to alleviate pain. Leeches were used to draw blood from people who were felt to be suffering from an excess of blood in the body.

Sometimes the affected area was cut with a knife. Both remedies were likely to leave the patient worse off.

Blood letting
From the *Luttrell Psalter* (English) *circa* 1325 - 1335 showing a practice which was commonplace in medieval England.

Mustard poultices made of bran, mustard and water were used to try to alleviate pains and inflammation in joints. Herbs were mixed with a little honey and applied to ulcers and sore throats and used to relieve pains in the stomach.

The most common cure for constipation was rhubarb, and while there is no evidence that Rothwell was then the great area for producing rhubarb that it is now, could it just be possible that the industry began at that time?

Who knows?

Doctors set great store by examining the urine of the patient, as this seemed to be an indication of the state of the 'humours' and what needed to be done to balance them. The body was believed to be made up of four elements of Earth, Air, Fire and Water, and for the body to remain healthy these ‘ humours’ should be in the correct proportion at all times.

Gradually, hospitals and schools of medicine were being established, but doctors were few and far between and their fees were so high that most people could not afford them. They had to rely on barbers instead of surgeons.

The Church banned doctors from dissecting dead bodies, so they were unable to find out how the body worked, thus progress to this end was slow.

Midwives had no training and were, in fact, merely older women most of whom had experienced childbirth themselves, which probably accounts for the high infant mortality rate.

When patients did not respond to treatment and death seemed to be imminent they were urged to bear pain stoically and confess their sins to a priest. When friends came to visit they would expect to be told what arrangements the patient wanted for a funeral and who was to inherit whatever possessions they had.

It was to be many years before there was understanding of the causes, transmission and cures for diseases. To this day there are people who still believe that, amongst other things, their health is ruled by the stars.

9. Medieval Food

ROTHWELL WAS A FAIRLY PROSPEROUS VILLAGE in the Middle Ages. The castle employed many local people, and the land was lush and green, allowing many varieties of vegetables and fruit to be grown both for local consumption and for trading at the market.

The landscape of England was very different from what it is today. There were some settlements of a good size, but mostly small towns and villages were dotted in between vast woodlands and forest areas.

Communication was very difficult. Messages took days or weeks to reach their destination. When it was necessary to travel journeys were mainly made on horseback. Horses had a major part to play in the lives of the lord of the manor and his household.

Naturally, hunting was very popular, both as a sport and for the procurement of meat for the dining table. At least once a week, and sometimes more, the huntsmen would ride out in search of deer, foxes and hares, in fact anything that would make a tasty dish for the Lord and his retinue, and sometimes even wild boar would be the prey.

This was a separate sport and had to be handled very carefully because boars were very dangerous. The dogs were taken out to the hunt wearing bells around their necks, to scare the boar and prevent them from hurting the dogs. Without this precaution the dogs would have been savaged and maybe even killed, so that a good days sport for the men and exercise for the horses might easily turn into a disastrous day for the hounds, to say nothing of the expense involved, and still no meat for the table.

The gamekeeper was usually kept busy hunting rabbits and pheasants, and there was always a stream nearby, as indeed there was in Rothwell, where trout and other fish could be caught and, if they were lucky enough to spot one, they might catch a salmon.

The water mill and fishponds

From the *Luttrell Psalter* (English) *circa* 1325 - 1335 and shows a water mill with millpond. It also shows the catching of eels in wicker fishing baskets. It can be said with some certainty that this would have happened at Rothwell. There was a mill on the site for 1000 years and with it a mill pond. There were also two fishponds, most certainly with eels in them.

Each Manor House had a home farm nearby, where the farmer tended a variety of animals. There were cows and goats for milk and meat, pigs provided pork and bacon, and sheep supplied wool as well as meat.

Of course, the creatures that no farmyard would be complete without were chickens. Eggs were a staple foodstuff in the kitchens of the rich, and the chickens themselves, along with ducks and geese, were often killed for the table on special feast days or at Christmas.

Sometimes even the poor people managed to own a pig or a cow between several of them and most had a few chickens, scrabbling around in the yard outside their hovels so that they would be able to make butter and cheese and collect the eggs. But these were very rarely for their own consumption and the women often walked miles to the nearest town on market days to sell the eggs, butter and cheese for a few coppers to spend on the other items they needed to survive.

If one of these peasants had a slightly larger house, he would be expected to give shelter to the communal pig, so perhaps he wasn't so lucky after all!

Harvesting acorn to feed swine
From the *Queen Mary Psalter* (English) *circa* 1310 – 1320 showing two men with clubs beating oak trees to knock down acorns for the pigs below to eat.

©British Library

Whatever the source of the animal, whether it was hunted and killed in the fields or slaughtered in the farmyard, it had to be preserved either by soaking in brine or smoking.

The animals that were killed at the hunt were often savaged by the dogs and some times were hit over the head to finish the job. The hounds were allowed to eat the entrails before the huntsmen bore the remaining meat home for preserving.

The farmyard animals had to be killed at the onset of winter because the amount of hay and acorns needed to feed them was just not available. The meat they provided was required to keep the household fed throughout the bad weather. The exception to this rule was that the beasts required for the breeding season the following spring would be spared.

The farmer often used a little psychology when it came to the slaughter of the pig. He would entice the animal with a bucket of acorns and while the pig's nose was in the trough, munching away, the farmer would gently stroke the pigs back to make him relaxed, then, with his other hand, he would hit him over the head with a hammer to stun him, and then slit his throat.

Killing and gutting pigs
From the *Queen Mary Psalter* (English) *circa* 1310 – 1320 showing a man killing a pig with the back of an axe while another cuts open a pig suspended by the hind legs. There is some evidence of sties for domesticated pigs on Stye Bank (*Sty Bank*, as it was called by the Saxons) which seems to indicate that pre Norman Rothwell also had domesticated swine.
©British Library

The notion was that a relaxed animal would produce much more tender meat!

The blood was caught, so that it could be used to make sausages, but the brains and tripe, which would not salt down were given to the servants to eat their fill. This was in contrast to the very meagre diet they usually had. There were probably a few sick servants around the next day!

Nothing was wasted. The wool was used for clothing and the animal skins would be cured to make footwear and saddles and other items for use with the horses. The pigs' bladders could be filled with air and sailed on the moat or in a stream, to see which one would go the farthest or they could be kicked around by the young boys – an early version of football perhaps?

The pigs' bladders could also be used by the peasants in their cauldron. They would be filled with either a savoury filling to make a kind of sausage (haggis?) or with a sweet filling such as pig fat, fruit and a little honey to make a sweet pudding which. would seem to be an early version of spotted dick – who knows?

Most of the countryside was owned by the King, who gave it, at his discretion, to some of his noblemen, as rewards for services rendered, (this was mainly getting troops together to fight whoever was trying to challenge his authority at any given time) or to knights he particularly favoured.

Of course they did not farm the land themselves but hired a farmer and farm labourers to do the job for them, for which they were rewarded with the use of a small strip of land in the village which they could cultivate for themselves, (an early version of an allotment perhaps) along with their small gardens.

This strip could be used to produce food for themselves and their families, and any excess could be sold either to others in the village or in the local town on market day.

The fields on the farms were used for growing cereals such as barley, wheat, corn and rye, and Rothwell was lucky enough to have it's own mill, where the cereals were taken to be ground into flour. This was a great saving on transport costs to the next available mill, and the economy grew as a consequence.

It was possible to grow grapes in most places, and Rothwell was no exception. It would seem as though the

Sowing seed

From the *Luttrell Psalter* (English) *circa* 1325 - 1335 showing a man sowing grain from a wattle sided wooden box, either side of which are crows, one feeding form a sack, the other being chased by a dog. In rural 14th century Rothwell this would have been a common sight.

©British Library

sun shone a bit more then than it does now! Some of the grapes were picked before they were ripe, deliberately, to be used in various recipes that required a sharp flavour. Once ripe, of course, they were trodden to a pulp and mixed with yeast to make wine.

The peasants grew various vegetables in their strips, according to the season of the year. These included beans, peas, onions, garlic, cabbages, and turnips, as well as many different kinds of herbs, which were very important, as they were used liberally in cooking as well as remedies for diseases.

The Lord of the Manor often gave permission for the young lads to collect berries from the hedgerows, and nuts from the trees in return for some small job on the estate. Some peasants also kept bees as honey was used for all sweetening purposes, including making the drinking water a little more palatable!

The harvest was a time for great rejoicing, assuming of course that it was a good harvest, and not a time of famine. If it was a bad harvest there would be no bread for the following year and the peasants would starve.

It was all hands on deck at harvest time to get the cereals gathered in during August or September before the weather changed and autumn winds and rain damaged the crop. The farmers carted the cereals to the mill, where the miller began work to grind it down to make flour, and from there it was taken to the bakery to make the bread.

Three distinct types of bread were baked. The superior, white bread, known as Manchet, was obviously reserved for the nobility. The ordinary people who lived in

Harvest Time
From the *Queen Mary Psalter* (English) *circa* 1310 – 1320 showing three men reaping the crop with the farmer directing them. This would have been a common sight in 14th century Rothwell.

the Manor House, including the servants ate the less refined brown bread.

The third type was a rough, dark, rye bread, which tasted very bitter and was often gritty from the sweepings from the floor of the granary. In the Manor House this was given to the animals. The peasants ate this third type and it was a large part of their basic staple diet, mostly for breakfast, washed down with ale.

The farmers took the barley from the fields to the brewery where it was processed and left to brew with yeast until it was ready to drink. It seems strange to us to think of drinking ale for breakfast, but it must have been quite weak or the peasants would have been drunk before the day's work started and that would never do. It was also more palatable than the water.

The farmers were quite into re-cycling, although they didn't know it as such. One of their main tasks was to supply manure for the fields belonging to the lord of the manor. To achieve this they would sweep the cowsheds, which had been lined with last year's straw, mix it with some earth and spread it over the roads and tracks in the village. It would be left long enough for a good many animals to walk over it and leave their droppings. The farmers would then collect it and take it back to the fields to be ploughed in. "Waste not want not" applied just as much then as it does today!

Ploughing with Oxen
From the *Luttrell Psalter* (English) *circa* 1325 - 1335 showing two men ploughing a field with yoked oxen. This would have been a common sight in 14th century Rothwell.

©British Library

In the manor house the main meal of the day was a very grand affair, and lasted for several hours. The lord and his family were seated at the top table, together with relatives and any distinguished guests while members of the household were seated at tables lower down.

The lord of the manor at his table
From the *Luttrell Psalter*, *circa* 1325 – 1335 showing the Lord of the manor eating at a trestle table with members of his family and clergy, a familiar sight in Rothwell Manor and even more grand when kings of England came to stay.

©British Library

The meal would begin with “frumenti”, which was a soup-like dish made of boiled, hulled wheat and almond milk, to which meat and spices had been added.

The next course would consist of four or five meat based dishes, some of which had been boiled and some roasted, together with a similar number of platters containing birds or fish and a variety dishes to tempt the palates of the lord and his guests.

One such 'novelty' was the top half of a chicken stitched to the bottom half of a small piglet and the resulting dish was called 'a cockatrice'.

The bigger the occasion, the more fancy the dishes, and surprises were the order of the day. Sometimes small birds were cooked for a short time, covered with pastry while still alive and when the pie was cut the birds flew around the room. It seems that:

Sing a song of sixpence
a pocketful of rye,
four and twenty blackbirds
baked in a pie
when the pie was opened
the birds began to sing
wasn't that a dainty dish
to set before the king.

wasn't just a nursery rhyme after all.

It's just as well the R.S.P.C.A wasn't around then; they would have been run off their feet!

The dessert consisted of any number of sweet dishes made from fruit, nuts, pastry, honey and marzipan, in various forms.

The *piece-de-resistance* was carried into the room shoulder high. It was often in the shape of flowers or a swan made of marzipan and, although it always looked good enough to eat, in fact it wasn't always edible; it was often just for show. This masterpiece of artistic delight was called a "subtlety" but it was anything but subtle!

The top table was served with all three courses, whereas the lower tables only had two. The servants only had one.

Soups were eaten with a spoon from a bowl, fashioned from wood or horn. The meat and dryer dishes were eaten from a trencher, which was a thick slice of dark, stale bread. It would soak up the juices and be eaten with the meal – hence saving on washing up, of course! It was eaten with the aid of a knife and fingers, as forks had yet to make an appearance.

The one thing missing from this sumptuous feast was vegetables of any kind, with the obvious exceptions of onions and garlic, as they were only considered to be fit for feeding to the animals and the peasants.

Onions and garlic, together with strongly flavoured herbs, were generally used in cooking to hide the 'off-flavours' of the meat.

However simple or elaborate the dish the lord would not partake of anything until it had been tasted by a trusted servant, just to be on the safe side. There was always someone plotting to try to take power or revenge, and he was often at risk, even within his own household.

The poor people had a mainly vegetarian diet. They could not afford to keep animals individually although sometimes a pig was shared, as indeed were most farm implements, and people helped each other out as and when required. The majority of the farm work was done by hand as no mechanical aids were available and after the peasants had done the work required by their lord and master, they were able to tend their own strip in which they also grew vegetables and herbs for flavouring.

Each household had a large cauldron, which was placed over the fire in the centre of the room, and this was filled with dried peas, water and any available vegetables, so long as they were not poisonous, and herbs.

Sometimes, if they were to hand, some scraps of bacon or a bone were added for flavour and this would boil for many hours until the mixture was thick and tasty. This meal was called 'potage', and, apart, from a chunk of bread for breakfast, was the only meal of the day.

Sometimes a chicken might find itself in the pot or a large sausage could be cooked in the pot at the same time, for a special occasion, but the usual daily meal was potage, so menus were not required!

Of course, the good English pick-me-up of a cup of tea was not available and the food was washed down with ale or water sweetened with a little honey.

To some extent, theirs was a good diet as it was low in fat and high in fibre, but this was greatly outweighed by the lack of vitamins, particularly A, C, & D and lead to many illnesses such as chesty coughs, colds and rickets.

The result of this difference in food intake was there for all to see. The wealthy were mostly overweight and likely to die early from strokes or heart disease brought on by eating too much fat. The peasants, on the other hand, were thin and hungry, and likely to die from malnutrition.

Many people today would like to lose a few pounds but, on the whole, most would rather live now than in The Middle Ages.

10. Law and Order - Crime and Punishment

BY THE TIME WILLIAM CONQUERED ENGLAND, after defeating Harold at Hastings, some laws and rights were already in place. The Anglo-Saxons (or as some people prefer Anglo-Scandinavians) had a very good democratic government ruled over by the king through his great earls and sheriffs.

The country was divided into shires and smaller communities such as Wapentakes* and manors. Each of these areas had its own court. If disputes could not be settled at a lower court, it went to a higher one.

When the Normans arrived they adopted the existing legal system, so far as it suited them, but as a reward for their loyalty the Norman knights who had fought with William were given lands of the Saxon lords, who, in some cases, worked well in conjunction with each other.

These lords were given the power to hold their own courts, known as Honour Courts as the land and surrounding areas were known as Honours. Locally in Rothwell it was the Honour of Pontefract.

One of the developments the Saxons had brought to the legal system was to produce written charters that could be referred to in court if necessary. William seemed to accept most of this system as it was, but he did change the punishments that he thought too harsh, for example, he substituted mutilation instead of beheading for murder,

---

* *Wapentake*, literally 'weapon touch'. A gesture of submission to authority.

and introduced a system of fines and seizure of property, goods or chattels. He also wanted his subjects to swear allegiance and loyalty to him.

He banned slavery!

Throughout the twenty years from Hastings to the production of the Domesday Book, Anglo-Saxon laws were prevalent until the Norman lords made their mark. It would seem that 'best practice' was the order of the day – incorporating rules and rights of both systems. Peace had to be kept as much as possible but still the authority of the king had to be paramount.

Uprisings did occur mainly in the West, North, and Wales, but these were ruthlessly put down by laying waste to many thousands of square miles.

The Church also played an important part in law and order in the community, basing its practices on biblical law, which was all-powerful. Ecclesiastical Courts had an important role in administering justice. The clerks (clerics) they provided to the law courts to record the proceedings supplemented their income by the fees that were paid.

At this time very few people were literate, even the men of some standing in the community, which meant that the clerks were a very valuable asset.

The Church, of course, in this context means abbeys, monasteries and cathedrals where Bishops' Courts were held and usually where archdeacons heard the cases.

The king, or a combination of ecclesiastical and royal lawyers, usually heard disputes between members of the upper hierarchy in the church. If this didn't work then the case could be referred to the Pope.

Because of the power of the Royal Courts and the common law throughout the land, the Barons felt they were losing their power. By the time John came to the throne they felt matters were getting worse for them.

John began increasing fees especially in land transfers where land was part of an inheritance. From John de Lacey he asked 7000 marks (approximately £4700) after he succeeded to the Manor of Pontefract. He had also been increasing the rents of his tenants and many were finding it difficult to keep body and soul together.

It was abuses of this kind that gave impetus to the imposition of the Magna Carta. One of the clauses suggested that a more reasonable sum for the transfer where a large inheritance was concerned. The sum should be related to the value of the property. In the case similar to that of John de Lacey a sum of £100 was considered more appropriate – clearly a big difference from the fee being asked by the king!

Manorial courts, of which Rothwell was a part within the Honour of Pontefract, were usually organised by the local Reeve, a manorial steward who looked after the day to day running of the manor. It was his job to gather together a group of men of good standing, usually twelve, to listen to the disputants and dispense justice.

If the case could be resolved before coming to court it would be a lot cheaper, but some cases could not be settled this way.

Land holding and transfers were often held in local courts, as were the cases of burglary, theft, violence and breach of the peace. On the death of a breadwinner the overlord took possession of all goods and chattels, leaving very little for the bereaved, who then had to work to gain sufficient funds to be able to buy them back.

The bereaved had to go to the manorial court to ask for items to be returned but a fee would have to be paid – maybe a pig or cheese or grain.

Very often disputes could be settled, either by the written law or local custom. The big advantage of this was that local knowledge of both the disputants and the local area made decisions easier, but if the wealthier members of the community were involved money could play an important part.

If the crimes were more serious or disputes more complicated the cases could be heard in a higher court, but this very often meant a fairly long wait. Local courts were usually held once a month, and shire courts about twice a year.

During the reign of Henry I this system seemed to work quite well. Unfortunately when Stephen came to the throne he became lax in ensuring the law was upheld, probably because he was trying to hold on to the throne against other claimants. At this time great lords and land-owners took advantage of the situation and took the law into their own hands. This often led to violence and corruption.

Following his accession, Henry II brought the law back under his own control as much as he could, reflecting the system as it was in Henry I's time. There were more written laws and charters, which made it difficult for the Earls and Barons to 'do their own thing'.

Henry wanted peace in the country and to enable the law to be consistent throughout the land he set up a 'Royal court' or Eyre. There were several eyres throughout the land, which may have had jurisdiction over several shires or counties. They were made up of educated men, very often in law, whom the king could trust. Probably two of these trustworthy men would be sent out to a shire 'capital' where they would have to find four others who had good standing in the area. These four then had to find more men until there were twelve good and trusty souls. This group of people, many of whom could have travelled many miles, incurred great expense, as they would also have had to find accommodation whilst they were sitting.

At least now the freemen of the country felt that they could get justice because if they felt justice had not been done at the lower court they could appeal to a higher one. The trouble was the king needed money and a fair amount of his income came from the legal system. It really had to pay for itself and some more!

Felons, whoever they were, had to pay fees, whether in cash or kind. Punishment at that time was quite brutal. Beheading, mutilation, the pillory were administered in public, bringing shame and humiliation not only to the convicted, but to their families as well.

It is understandable why criminals fled to the forest or were sent there as punishment i.e. outlawed.

Collecting acorns for the swine

Gathering the corn

A wild boar

The lord of the manor at his table

The carriage of

Hunting with dogs

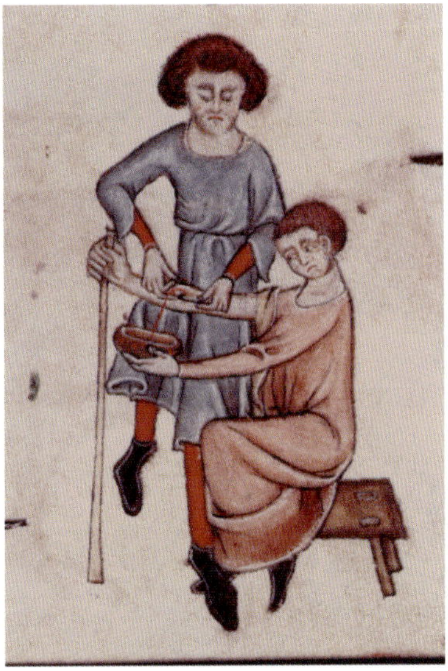

Blood letting

the royal princesses

Water mill and fishpond

Sowing the seed

Ploughing with oxen

11. Religion

WHEN THE DOMESDAY BOOK WAS COMPILED IN 1086, after the Norman Conquest of England in 1066, for the purpose of determining what was of value in the country, no church building was recorded in Rothwell. This may have been because it was extremely small and poor and not deemed to be worth recording.

It might have meant that a preaching stone was in use. This would be a large stone, usually on rising ground, which would be used as a meeting point by a wandering friar, probably from Nostell Priory or Kirkstall Abbey, both of which had been endowed by Ilbert de Lacey of Pontefract castle and lord of the manor of Rothwell. The friar would set up his Holy Rood, often a silver cross mounted on a pole, and this would be Rothwell Church for the day.

One explanation for the origin of the name 'Rothwell' is 'Rood' and 'Well' – the church by the well. The first mention of Rothwell Church in the official records occurs in a Charter granted by Henry II between 1154 and 1158 which confirms the gift of six churches to the canons at Nostell Priory in 1130 by Hugh de Laval, who was the Patron of the church and tenant of the Manor of Rothwell under Robert de Lacey of Pontefract castle, his superior Lord.

Early churches were built in the same way as the cottages of the villagers, of wattle and daub or of wood, and would be quite small because village populations were not very large. As populations grew and more land was developed, churches were enlarged.

Another reason why they were enlarged was to accommodate a number of chapels or altars within the church building.

Using local stone left over from the building of the castle, built to facilitate the King's hunting, Rothwell Church would eventually become well established. There is evidence for a stone bridge connecting the castle to the church over the great cut way (Wood Lane).

There is an early stone *piscina* near the altar of the present church and several stones which date from Saxon times before the Conquest.

Also in the present church is an ancient coat, known locally as John of Gaunt's waistcoat, dating from about the time the castle was in use. In Batty's history of Rothwell he states,

> *This undergarment is made of strong, coarse canvas, well and truly padded with sheep's wool. It consists of several layers about three quarters of an inch thick and quilted with twine. It has armholes but without sleeves.*

Some research has been undertaken on this by experts at the Royal Armories in Leeds and we will learn more about their conclusions at a later date.

The parish church was served by a priest appointed by the founder, or patron of the church. There was a right of patronage attached to the glebe, which was a piece of land given to the church. This could be inherited by the successors and descendants of the appointed priest.

Today, in some cases, the lord of the manor, as patron still 'appoints' the vicar of the church, usually known as ‘rector’, as he is responsible for the incumbent’s stipend (wages).

Peasants who lived in Rothwell would be expected to provide their service to the lord of the manor and also their obligations to their local church. The clerk in Holy Orders was appointed by the lord of the manor but the parishioners were expected to supply all his needs. All his food and clothing would have to be provided as well as equipment for services .

The parishioners were taxed to support the church and its incumbent. They had to pay tithes (one tenth) of their corn and other crops, of the increase of their livestock and even of their garden produce. Most of this was given to the Lord of the manor and he would decide how much of this was to be dedicated to support the living of the incumbent. The records show that, even into modern times the people of Rothwell had to deliver two gallons of milk each day to the church door. The vicar was expected to sell this to supplement his income.

The payment of tithes dates from the Old Testament and was adopted by Western Christian churches, but never by the Eastern Orthodox churches. It was enforced in Europe by secular law from the 8th century and it was not repealed in England till 1936, the last country in Europe to do so.

Villagers' families also had to render up their second best beast when a relative died in recompense for the tithes the deceased could be assumed to have concealed in his lifetime. All made oblations at mass on the great feast days and at weddings, baptisms and funerals.

Parishioners were called upon to keep the nave of the church in good repair. This provided a substantial indoor space and would be used by the villagers as a communal meeting place for secular as well as religious purposes. They also had to keep the churchyard in good order and provide many items of equipment: bells for the steeple; a pyx, which is a small box, generally made of a precious metal, in which the consecrated Host (elements for Holy Communion) is reserved or carried to the sick; a font for Baptisms; a bier for the dead; a vessel for Holy water. Among the other items would be a lenten veil, which seems to have been a large piece of material which could be fastened to screen off the Chancel during Lent. (Statues and representations of the Cross are still veiled in purple cloth in Lent in Rothwell Church today.)

There were periodic visitations by officials of the diocese or the religious houses and the surviving records of these frequently revealed buildings that were in disrepair, and equipment and ornaments broken, old, worn-out or missing. (These 'visitations' continue today in the form of 'quinquennials', i.e., every five years.)

The priest's duty was to say or sing the mass daily. He was required to administer the sacraments to his parishioners, to see that they made their confessions before Holy Communion and take note of their attendance at church. He had to pay due attention to the needs of the sick and to see that they made their wills at the proper time and in the proper legal form. The Last Will and Testament came within the province of the church's law and to die intestate amounted to a spiritual offence.

In the earliest part of our period, around the 12th century, when the head of a household died, everything he had was deemed to belong to the Lord of the Manor and was forfeited on his death. – *All the pigs, goats, mares at grass, and his horse, all his bees, all his uncut bacons, all his cloth of wool or flax, the best ox, and his brass pots and whatever can be found of gold or silver.*

His dependants would have to seek an audience with the lord of the manor and beg him for enough of these to allow them to carry on. He would probably allow this in the interest of keeping his workforce from starvation, but we can be sure he would keep anything of value.

There were penalties for non compliance with the church law or religious practice, for example, non-attendance at church on Easter Sunday, for adultery or even for spending too long in the alehouse. Wrongdoers could find themselves presented before the congregation and have to confess in public or, in more serious cases, before the ecclesiastical court. They could be fined or made to do penance. They could be excommunicated, which meant they were barred from receiving the sacraments and from burial in consecrated ground.

An offender might be absolved by a priest (in extreme cases only by a Bishop or the Pope) and received back into the Church after confessing their sin and doing penance for it.

The concept of community was very important as all had to work together to survive. The village community and the church community were one and the same. Religion played a major role in everyday life and the year would be regulated round the various Christian festivals.

In a time when communities' hold on their lands could be precarious, Rogation Sunday, six weeks after Easter, was when parson and parishioners went around the parish boundaries, beating the ground with sticks to denote possession and ask God's favour on the land and the harvest, was extremely important. They were very dependant on good weather for a good harvest which would see them through the winter and God's blessing was needed to ensure success in every part of the farming system or famine and death could easily result. The word "Rogation" comes from the latin *rogare* – to ask.

The Feast of All Saints (1st November) marked the start of winter when cattle were brought into the byre, as well as the time when evil spirits abroad on Hallowe'en had to be propitiated.

The twelve days of Christmas were the first long holiday (holy-day) after the autumn ploughing and the sowing of winter grain – the holiday ending with Epiphany (6th January).

Plough Monday, the next after Candlemas (2nd February, the Presentation of Christ in the Temple – traditionally the time when money was collected to provide the candles for the church for the next twelve months), was when the spring ploughing began. This task, if luck and the weather held, was over by Easter, which began another holiday lasting to Hock day, two Tuesdays later.

Fallow ploughing, weeding the corn,and sheep shearing filled the time to midsummer (the Feast of the Nativity of St. John the Baptist, 24th June) which was the traditional beginning of haytime, just as the feast of St. Peter *ad vincula* or St Peter in chains (1st August) was the beginning of harvest. The latter was more popularly known as 'Lammas Day' (from the Old English *hlaf-maesse* – 'loaf mass'), possibly pointing to a custom of bringing loaves made from the new wheat to the church to be blessed.

By Michelmas (29th September), again given luck and good weather, the harvest was gathered and St. Michael's feast could coincide with Harvest Home, the end and crown of the farming year. It was also the time when the autumn work in the fields began again making Michelmas the start and end of the 'eternal agricultural cycle'.

By absorbing into its calendar many of the traditional festivals of the agricultural community the church gave these festivals new meaning and helped to fuse the community of parishioners with the community of the village.

In a time when most people were illiterate, the church calendar gave structure to people's lives. Appointments could be made with regard to certain saints' days, and, for example, an agreement could be made to repay a debt by, say, St. Agnes' Eve

The community as a whole was expected to attend church every Sunday and on Saints' days. The service was spoken in Latin by a priest who might, or might not, understand what he was intoning, depending how much education he had. Many priests simply learnt it by rote and recited it, others simply mumbled something, hence *mumbo-jumbo.* The congregation would scarcely have noticed the difference.

Churches would be decorated inside with paintings depicting stories from the Bible; visual aids to help the people's understanding of what they were meant to believe. Most churches had a 'Doom Painting' in a prominent place which depicted 'The Last Judgement', when Christ would return in Glory and receive the Good into Heaven and consign the wicked to the flames of Hell.

> *Men learned by eye and ear and lessons so learned were mainly expressed in emotions whether fear of hell, hope of salvation, thankfulness or humility.*

Monasteries had been founded both before and after the Conquest, sometimes as a thanksgiving for victory in battle, thanksgiving for recovery from illness or as a penance for sins committed. Ilbert de Lacey had founded Kirkstall Abbey and Nostell Priory and they were often receiving gifts to help their upkeep, such as the churches given to Nostell Priory by Hugh de Laval. The churches were Rothwell, Ackworth, Featherstone, South Kirkby, Huddersfield and Batley. The gift does not imply that he gave a building to the canons; there would have been no advantage in this as they would have had to maintain it.

He freely transferred to them his right of patronage together with all profits arising from it and in return they would remember him in their prayers during his life and after his death.

Nostell Priory continued for more than a century to present rectors to Rothwell. By this system the Priory eventually controlled large amounts of valuable property for which it paid no service but prayers.

The monks held their lands and had a similar system in place to support them as did the lords of the manor, namely duties of service of the peasants who lived on their land. They would be expected to provide food for the monks or manual labour for the monks to grow their own.

Some manors would be assigned to provide cash for the monks' clothing and the peasants would find they had to work on their service to the monks before being able to grow food for their families.

Monastic estates were extended and more land was brought into cultivation by making compact granges. These could be obtained by clearing uninhabited areas or by depopulating a village to accommodate it.

The first recorded incumbent of Rothwell church was William Blundell who was instituted on August 4th 1242. He did not live in Rothwell and was a deputy canon of St. Paul's Cathedral in London. This meant he would have to appoint someone to look after the spiritual needs of the parish. He could hire a chaplain, who was an unbeneficed priest (a priest without a 'living'), who would look after it in return for a small stipend. The bulk of the profit would remain with the absent incumbent. Or a vicar could be appointed who would have greater security of tenure and could be expected to do a better job of looking after his interests. In this case the vicar held his 'cure' as a freehold benefice, to which he was presented, instituted and inducted and from which he could only be removed by death, voluntary resignation – or conviction of a serious, criminal offence!

His vicarage was a fixed endowment formed by the assignation to him and his successors of a portion of the revenues of the church. In 1253 William Blundell presented Roger of Warwick to the vicarage with the assent of his patrons, the prior and convent of St. Oswalds. Roger was instituted by Archbishop Gray at his manor house at Scrooby in Nottinghamshire on 1 July 1253.

The endowment of the vicarage is specified as consisting of: the Altarage, i.e. the offerings of the parishioners and fees for marriages, burials etc., and of the tithe of hay throughout the parish except that arising from the "demesne" i.e. the land belonging to the Lord of the manor and cultivated by his villeins.

The rest of the fruits of the church, including the great tithe of corn remained in the possession of the rector, William Blundell.

In 1270 the vicar of Rothwell was John of Selston who obtained from Archbishop Giffard leave to go on a pilgrimage and be away for five years, receiving in the meantime the proceeds of the vicarage provided that he arranged for the celebration of Divine Service in his church.

We are not told whether he returned or not.

The church taught that, after death the soul must spend time in purgatory to prepare for Heaven and, as this was time spent in pain to atone for past sins, people wanted to make sure that their time there was as short as possible. They could obtain 'indulgences' from the church by giving alms, making a pilgrimage, endowing a monastery etc., and they would be remitted so many days, weeks, years. No wonder they wanted to make sure people prayed for their souls after their death.

Much of the festivity of medieval England was organised by the craft guilds Most required members to perform certain duties such as attend the Guild Mass and the funerals of members. Guilds were mutual insurance societies for this life and the life to come. Funds were used to provide benefits to members who suffered disaster or destitution. Living members of the Guilds prayed for the souls of those who had passed on knowing that others in turn would pray for them. Deceased members of families could be enrolled in the Guilds so that members could pray for their souls.

Churches had more than one altar to meet the demand for masses for special groups or individuals, and Rothwell was no exception. People often bequeathed legacies to be spent, sometimes on a lavish scale, on masses for their souls. There was a very large class of unbeneficed priests who found a living serving altars of churches and celebrating masses for the departed.

Rothwell had two such chantries in the Middle Ages and one later, in 1523. The chantry of Our Lady in the south aisle was founded by John Radclive in 1329. A second chantry of Our Lady, probably in the north aisle, was founded by William Scargill in 1494.

The decree of Archbishop Melton confirming the first of these, dated 11th July 1329 survives in his register at York.

From the preamble -

And so our beloved son Sir John of Radclive perpetual vicar of the Holy Trinity of Rothwell of our diocese, desiring while he has the light, to walk more securely among his fellows and, while the course of this brief life is disturbed by the miseries of his flesh, to provide more carefully, with the favour of God's mercy, for the salvation of his soul, has willed, with the consent of the prior and convent of St. Oswald of Nostell who hold the said church in appropriation to their uses, and are the patrons of the vicarage of the same, to cause to be ordained at his own expense, a chantry to be celebrated for all time at the altar of St. Mary in the said church of Rothwell, out of the devotion which he ever cherishes for the salvation of the soul of dame Alice de Lacey, sometime Countess of Lincoln, and for the salvation of the souls of those others who are herein written.

All Chantries were abolished at the Reformation, along with Indulgences, when King Henry VIII broke with Rome and declared himself to be the Head of the Church of England.

As a footnote, showing how the ancient ways continued into modern times, there is an interesting anecdote in Manley's *A Short History of Rothwell.*

> *Just before the First World War Mr. Fred Hirst, acting for the firm of John Farrar of Oulton, was sitting in the Unicorn at Carlton receiving tithe payments, when a youngish man brought in his notice and said "Ah weant pay". An old man who had paid and was drinking his customary bonus pint said to him "Thee pay. I remember when I wor a lad, t'parson's cart come to the Three Tailed Acre* [a field in the angle of Matty Lane and Leadwell Lane] *for his sheaves. T'farmer refused to let him have them. T'Parson's man turned everyone out of the field, shut the gate, tied it with red tape and sealed it. "Corn mun rot" he said "Brak t'seal who dares" If they could seal t'field up then they can seal thee up nah. "Thee pay."*

The young man paid !

12. Markets and Fairs

WHEN DID ROTHWELL BECOME A MARKET TOWN?

According to Batty's *History of Rothwell*,

> *'John De Lacy obtained a privilege for all merchants coming by water to Pontefract to be toll free, knowing that undue restrictions on trade and commerce were hurtful to a commercial people.'*

John De Lacy died in 1240 leaving two daughters and an only son Edmund.

The Rothwell people applied to Edmund De Lacy to get him to induce the king to grant them the privileges of a market town.

He succeeded on the terms as follows:

> *35th year of Henry III's reign* [1250] *The king hath granted for the ease and profit of the lieges and tenants of our town of Rothwell within the Honor of Pontefract, at their request, a certain market within the town aforesaid upon a Wednesday and two fairs there, to wit, one of them on the Eve and Day of St Thomas the Martyr* [July 7th] *and the other on the Eve and Day of St Matthew the Evangelist* [September 21st].

The granting of two fairs a year shows that Rothwell at this time was considered commercially important, indeed more important than Leeds, as it was one of the administrative centres for the Honour of Pontefract.

The record shows that in the 30th year of Henry III's reign a tallage (an arbitrary tax imposed on the royal tenants, boroughs and demesne lands) was assessed by which Pontefract paid 103½ marks, the burgh of Leeds 3½ marks and Rothwell 4½ marks. [A mark at this time was 13s 4d. For ease of modern comparison 5p is the same as 1shilling. There were 20 shillings in a pound and 12d (pennies) in a shilling. Originally the pound meant a pound weight of silver.]

The two fairs would become great occasions for the people of Rothwell. They would be eagerly anticipated as a change from their dull everyday lives; an opportunity to make and renew acquaintance with people who came from much further afield, and a chance to acquire goods which would not normally be available locally.

Each fair lasted two days, making it worth while for merchants who may have had to spend considerable time travelling here. There would be dancing and feasting and all kinds of entertainment on offer.

Merchants at this time were bringing in goods from all over Europe and beyond. England had trade links with the Baltic and Scandinavian countries and goods were imported through the East coast ports from Hull to Ipswich.

In 1217 and 1237 the Norwegians and Swedes made trade treaties with England and the sea route to the Mediterranean was fully open well before 1349 enabling goods from that region to be brought by sea to Yorkshire.

The wealthier lords required various merchandise that could not be produced locally, not only luxurious garments and materials but fine tableware and other rarities to satisfy their prestigious needs.

More ordinary articles could also be provided by the merchants who plied the waterways and land routes: the seas of Southern and Northern Europe, the great rivers and, on occasion, the roads inherited from Roman times were used as commercial arteries.

In his *Colloquy*, the English abbott, Aelfric (early 11th Century) describes the various professions.

The merchant is quoted as saying

> *I am useful to the king, the noble, the wealthy man and the whole population. I board a ship with my goods and I navigate to the lands beyond the sea.I sell merchandise and acquire precious things that are not found here in our land. I transport them at great risk and sometimes I am shipwrecked, losing all I have and only barely escaping with my life.*

The evidence shows wool and grain could be exported in bulk.

> *On the Lacy estates in Yorkshire, the constable of Pontefract castle gathered up the wool from the manors and sold it in bulk for a sum , which in 1305 totalled £116. The advantage to merchants over buying, in penny packets, wool of doubtful and varying quality is obvious enough.*

The creation of markets and fairs, either by means of royal grants, or by the action of more locally based interested parties, reached a climax in the 13th century. Throughout England by 1300 there was a network of chartered and locally founded markets and fairs. The charter simply recognised the legal right of a community to hold a market.

Many markets were held without a charter, so the granting of a charter did not necessarily lead to the creation or expansion of a market area. The records show that between 1227 and 1350 the Crown granted market rights to more than 1200 places in England and Wales, indicating an intense interest in trade and profitable possibilities.

In Saxon burghs, where defence was a major consideration, as it may have been in Rothwell to keep the person of the King safe on his visits, no permanent market areas seem to have been provided within town plans. Trade was largely conducted in churchyards and open areas.

At this time there was a close relationship between the church and the market place. Markets were often held on Sundays until the late 13th century, but in 1285 the statute of Winchester ordered that,

> *Henceforth neither fairs nor markets be kept in churchyards for the honour of the church.*

From about this time the records show a considerable number of new market places appearing in towns, and in some cases the main street may have been widened to allow for this.

Many market areas had a cross erected in a prominent position. This could have been symbolic of the sanction of religion to encourage honesty. It would also provide a focal point for the people to meet and a preaching place outside the church.

The market was a trading place where town and country people congregated but it was also a place of supervision and regulation. It was necessary to provide enough space for free movement while at the same time creating access and exit points which could be controlled and where tolls could be collected. It was logical for the authorities eventually to urge the replacement of canvas stalls with tiled 'shoppa' as the lord, or controller of the market, realised that it was in his interest to have permanent, rather than temporary market stalls.

Today, Rothwell Market Cross is situated outside the Health Centre. This is a modern copy of the Medieval cross which stood nearby which was damaged by a vehicle many years ago. Its replacement was sited as closely as possible to the known site of the original cross.

So, what would be on sale in the weekly market on Wednesdays in Rothwell in the 12th and 13th centuries when the hunting park was in use and the king could be expected to visit?

In the peasants' eyes, their holdings should provide their families with adequate supplies of food and drink but there were other needs that they could not supply and they would need to buy these: shoes and clothing, salt, pots for the kitchen, implements and tools and perhaps some fish to supplement their diet.

To obtain the money they needed peasants would sell some of their excess produce. Consequently they would frequent the market as buyers and sellers.

On a half virgate of land a peasant might keep a cow, a few sheep and a pig The cow and sheep might provide a little milk butter and cheese. Wool and dairy produce would be sold to obtain the means to buy what was needed, but the bulk of the money would come from the sale of grain.

All labour services were commuted into money rents in 1327, so the peasant needed to raise money to pay his dues as well. Consequently he had to organise his land so that it could produce a marketable surplus.

In Rothwell, being a pleasant wooded valley, timber and brushwood might provide a welcome addition to the sale of a few livestock, poultry and eggs, cider or garden crops. Great care would have to be taken to make sure these were taken from outside the hunting park or severe penalties would be imposed.

Some buyers in the market might be town craftsmen who needed wool or hides or imported wood to carry on their crafts. There would be rural and urban customers for goods made in the town – cloth, made up garments, earthen pots and wooden dishes, spades and cartwheels, ladders and baskets.

From their earliest years women spun, wove, sewed and embroidered ceaselessly and many poor women tried to balance meagre budgets by what they could earn from 'women's work'.

So could the peasants in Rothwell afford the prices that were being asked in their market?

Prices responded dramatically to harvests, dear when the harvest was poor, cheaper when the harvest had been more plentiful. Livestock epidemics would send up the price of animals. The price of wool responded to government intervention in the export trade or the weight of taxes on it.

Prices tended to rise when a surge of clipped coinage came into circulation and to fall when the proper currency was restored. When coins were made of solid silver small pieces could be clipped from the edge and, if enough of these were collected, they could be melted down and new coins made.

This practice was counteracted in due course by 'milling' coins, i.e., minting them with a ribbed edge.

Some idea of the peasant's ability to pay may be seen from setting the prices of consumer goods against wages.

In the generations around 1300, an unskilled labourer (provided he could find work) might earn 1 to 1½d. per day. Salt may have been relatively plentiful and shoes could be bought for around 2d. per pair, but the cheapest cloth on the market (russet and blanket) cost 1s. to 1s. 6d. a yard. A simple smock, therefore, could involve the expenditure of from two to four months' earnings and it is not surprising that, in the inventories of the richer peasants, even worn robes are given a value which may be 3s. or more. Candles were dear at 1½d. to 2d. per pound. Pepper cost 1s. per pound and this must have encouraged them to collect wild herbs to add flavour to their food.

In the on-line gazetteer of markets and fairs in England and Wales to 1516, the entry for Rothwell, West Yorkshire, states that the market charter was granted on the 6th February 1408 by King Henry IV. A market was to be held weekly on Wednesday and two fairs a year on the vigil and feast day of Thomas the Martyr (July 7th) and vigil and feast day of Matthew the Evangelist (21st September).

13. The Cost of Medieval Living

IT MAY BE OF INTEREST TO THE GENERAL READER to consider some of the earnings and expenses of the residents of Rothwell in the Middle Ages.

Fortunately some records of accounts have survived and these are summarised in the next few pages.

1322

Thomas Deyvill was keeper of the lands of contrariants in Yorkshire. His accounts for the period 24th March to 29th September 1322 show rents paid by individuals as well as bond tenants – bonded to the manor – and also tenants of the manor by ancient custom. Maybe these people were descended from the original Anglo-Saxon owners of the land.

As well as money collected as rent, produce was also recorded, sometimes in fine detail, e.g. 320 eggs sold at Easter for 1s. 4d.

Rent was paid for animal grazing in the park, fishery and even for a dove house. Notably, rent was not paid on un-repaired property, for example, the fulling mill at 'Oldeton' because it was broken and had not been re-paired.

There was no record of payment for honey, wax, herons and firewood because there wasn't any!

Extra rent was charged for constructing a forge 'to make iron' which required tree roots and trunks being grubbed out of the ground for the fire.

One man, Robert Shorte, rented Rothwell Park for 16 weeks at 30 shillings per week. He wasn't charged for feast days which included Easter, Whitsuntide and three other days. In total Mr Shorte was charged £21. 15s. It is to be hoped he thought it worthwhile and made a profit from the iron. The accounts note that a plough made with six pieces of his iron, plus the wages of a smith, cost 3s. 7d.

There were other uses for iron, most notably shoes 'for cart-beasts and plough-beasts', also for horses used by stewards, etc. of the Lord of the Manor.

The total of receipts for this six month period was £62, 2 shillings and 8 pence farthing. (A farthing was a quarter of a penny).

Although we think of medieval peasants as working for next to nothing, wages were paid depending on the skills employed. As most of the villagers were very poor the extra income was most welcome.

Some of the bondmen and cottars were paid in kind. It is noted that 200 herring were paid for reaping the lord's crops and one quart of rye was given for bread, which made 120 loaves. This was the equivalent of giving the peasants half a loaf per day.

Of course, with ownership of property goes the responsibility of maintenance. It was no different in the 14th century. Not only did buildings have to be kept in good repair but also farm equipment and animal welfare had to be taken into consideration.

Under the heading of 'Repairs' it is shown that maintenance was an on-going occupation and there is an entry for 'new making a window in the north side of the great chamber, with pintles and gudgeons and nails, roofing the chamber over the window with 500 spikings, 300 great brads to lay the shingles and 2 keys for the doors, 4 shillings and 8 pence.'

This would appear to have been quite a large window. Were the keys for the locks on the windows? Was this evidence of security even then!

Under this same heading every repair imaginable seems to be listed: repairs to buildings, obtaining mill-stones, wages to men breaking stones in quarries.

Repairs done were checked, i.e. counted and the payments made for those works, whether in kind or cash.

The bridge to the manor was repaired and men were employed to keep watch around the park – day and night – for 15 days to prevent anyone entering the park during the King's stay there.

Also recorded are the tithes to the prebendaries (canons who received tithes as stipend) of the chapel of St. Clement, Pontefract and also the vicar of Rothwell. During the Whitsuntide Term this was paid in cash – 16s. 8d. for 6 months.

The cost of ropes, wages for ploughing, payment to men fetching forfeited sheep and pigs to Rothwell, pitch and blood to anoint the sheep; shearing and preparing wool was recorded. Liveries (payments) to men looking after livestock, making new gates and mending the fencing around the park, making hedges, wages to women removing and cleaning forage from the great barn to the cow house and cleaning the barn for the 'King's hall to be held there' were also noted.

Mentioned is made that the tenement of John de Methal of Oldton is in the King's hands because of its forfeiture for Whitsuntide Term. This cost the manor 5s.

This seems to have been some kind of punishment because the next entry is 'sum of unpaid rent and expenses:- £27.7s.1½d. and he owes £34.15s.6¾d.

A stock-take was done at the Grange, usually the main farm (probably Rothwell) attached to castle, and some of the wheat was given to the reeve for expenses incurred. Silage was shared, but because corn was so expensive at this time several people took their liveries in cash and sometimes in bread. Oats were sown on 25 acres of land.

Four draught animals, oxen, were found at the Manor but other animals – sheep and pigs – were brought there from outlying farms, as were fleeces and hides. One entry notes that one animal was stolen by persons unknown on the King's arrival. Several also died from 'murrain' – a plague-like disease.

Finally, the acreage and whether it was under cultivation, fallow or left as meadow for hay were listed.

The following are subsidiary entries.

24th March 1322 – 29th September 1322: Thomas Deyvill, keeper of the Castle and honour of Pontefract challenged the charge of 13s. 4d. (67p in current money) for rent for the farm of the fulling mill at Olton, which is part of the Manor of Rothwell, because the mill was carried away by a flood (probably the previous year) and not repaired. But then, sometime after on 5th April, he paid £33 9s 3¾d from the Manor of Rothwell.

29th September 1322 – 29th September 1323. Rec'd from Thomas Deyvill from the Manor of Rothwell £34 4s 1d.

29th September 1323 – 20th May 1324. Rec'd from Thomas Deyvill from Manor of Rothwell £20 1s 11d.

Thomas Deyvill was still keeper at Pontefract on 16th March 1327 and collecting rents and tithes. One entry says that 'a messuage and 60 acres in Carlton are in the kings hands because John, the son and heir of Robert le Hunt, is 19 years old and not yet of age so the land has been let to Robert de Knousthorp'. This was sometime after 29th September 1326.

Every purchase made and monies paid out are recorded:

A new sack	*9d.*
2 dung forks	*2d.*

The tithes to the prebendaries and the Vicar of Rothwell continued to be paid.

The reeve was paid 3s. 4d. for overlooking all of this work. In fact he seemed to run the whole show!

In September 1326 Edward II had been captured and imprisoned. His wife, Isabella, was acting as ruler until Edward 'abdicated in favour of his son Edward III' and it could be that the Queen was staying at Pontefract.

There are one or two entries relating to Thomas Devill, the Queen's Keeper, and the delivery of wheat, oats, three draught animals, crops growing in the ground, hay and dead stock.

14. The Decline and Fall of Rothwell Castle

WHILE JOHN OF GAUNT WAS ALIVE, Rothwell Castle was a favourite place for the nobility to visit. It was probably looked after by a 'Reeve' – a steward answerable to the lord at Pontefract Castle.

At the time of John's death in February 1399, Richard II was on the throne and in retaliation for the disputes between himself and Henry Bolingbroke, John of Gaunt's son, he sent men and soldiers to attack and destroy Rothwell Castle, stripping it of its treasures and knocking down the walls and fences.

The unfortunate reeve, John of Rothwell, and his daughter, Lady Rose, had no chance! Part of the destruction was the demolition of the bridge from the castle to the church, over what we now know as Wood Lane. One report suggests the reeve was killed by a falling stone but Brown (900 yrs after Doomsday) indicates that he protested at the destruction and also the rough treatment of his daughter and that is why he was killed.

Bolingbroke had designs on the crown. Richard II was an unstable, weak king. His mood swings brought him into conflict with his barons and parliament and, in 1386, Richard was deprived of most of his power by parliament who appointed a commission to oversee the government.

Richard was greatly displeased and with a small band of men tried to regain control, but was defeated. Several of his friends were convicted of treason.

Richard then promised that he would be more amenable and his authority was restored.

Now it was his turn to take revenge! Many of his enemies were executed. Others were imprisoned or exiled and their estates seized, which was the fate of Henry Bolingbroke when his father, John of Gaunt, died.

Richard acquired much wealth from the confiscated estates and, with his followers, decided to take his armies to Ireland, which he could now afford to do.

With Richard out of the way his enemies seized the opportunity to act.

Henry returned from France after only four months exile, landed in the Humber estuary and gathered an army. His main supporters were the Percy family (Earl of Northumberland), and the Neville family (Earl of Westmoreland).

Richard returned in haste and lost many loyal friends against this 'army'. Of the large army he had set out with only about 100 remained. It was a disaster!

He took refuge in Conway Castle.

Richard now realised his was a lost cause and soon surrendered to Henry. Eventually in September 1399, seven months after John of Gaunt had died, the king signed a deed of abdication and gave the crown to Henry who placed it on his head and declared himself Henry IV.

He was the first of the Lancastrian kings.

Richard was confined in various castles, but mainly at Pontefract. Could it be that Rothwell Castle had been made habitable again and this was one of the castles in which he was incarcerated?

Henry was crowned in late 1399 and Richard died in Pontefract Castle the following year in circumstances yet to be conclusively explained.

The early part of Henry's reign was troubled with former allies becoming enemies. It wasn't until 1408, when the Earl of Northumberland was killed at Bramham Moor, that Henry could feel secure on his throne.

Throughout this time men from towns and villages were called upon to fight. In Rothwell their allegiance should have been with the king given their association with his family.

There would be no time or money available for these men to tend their land – that would be left for the women and those not fit to fight.

Who would take on the responsibility to restore and rebuild the castle and make it a *hospitium* again?

Parliament was constantly in dispute with Henry about taxes and customs dues as his expenses were getting out of hand. He also had an illness that kept recurring, which was thought at the time to be leprosy, and was another drain on the treasury.

After Henry's death in 1413 his son, the Prince of Wales became king as Henry V.

Again money was an issue! Was it ever thus? Places like Pontefract Castle would have had to be kept in good order but Rothwell would suffer. The only thing that it seemed to be good for was the timber, which could be used for repairing fences and building houses, and the scrub for firewood. The local mills would need substantial planks of wood to shore up the banking of the mill race. Outbuildings always need shingles for roofing.

Although Rothwell had been an important administrative centre, after the plague the population had diminished and the old order had changed in so far as the peasants now had more power.

Henry V was more interested in conquering France to regain the lands lost during the previous reigns. Apart from the manorial courts and the justice they dispensed, Henry would have had no interest in Rothwell. His grandfather, John of Gaunt, had, supposedly, killed the last wild boar in the north of the country so there was not really any more exciting sport to be had hereabouts.

As it happened, Henry V was a lot better at looking after the royal finances than his predecessors, but the wars in France were still taking a lot of money. At this time four-year-old Richard, son of the disgraced Earl of Cambridge, heir of the Earl of March, whom many saw as the rightful heir to the crown, became a Royal Ward and was brought up at both Pontefract Castle and Methley Hall, which is about a mile and a half away from Rothwell.

Richard's guardian at Methley was the royal retainer, Robert Waterton, whose descendants built a house on the outskirts of Wakefield known as Waterton Hall. (Very popular for weddings today.)

Was Methley now the new Rothwell?

Henry VI, who inherited the throne in 1422 when he was nine months old, was brought up by nobles nominated by his father. For the first few years of his life he was mainly under the care of his mother away from the main court, but eventually he was provided with tutors who had strict instructions to treat him as any other young nobleman at that time.

He grew up to be a very pious young man, but again France was the problem. All he wanted was peace there.

All resources from the treasury seemed to be swallowed up by this conflict and the north of England was virtually left to its own devices.

When the king became ill with, what we now know as schizophrenia, the queen, Margaret of Anjou, ruled in his stead and she was a very strong woman! As far as she was concerned the lands in France that had been lost to the English crown must be re-conquered at all costs, mainly because these were areas of France that brought a lot of money into England through the wine and wool trades.

By this time many farms were now in ruin as nearly all the available workforce was away fighting. These holdings were turned over to sheep. The wool brought in a considerable amount of money and was far less labour intensive than farming; fewer labourers were needed.

The peasants were now able to sell their labour on the open market and with their earnings they were able to buy their small plots of land and any others they could afford.

Sheep were becoming big business! By this time also, because of a lack of male heirs to the dukedoms and earldoms, many inheritances were passed down through the female line. Many of the male heirs had either been killed in wars, feuds, the plague, and even tournaments, leaving a very depleted male population.

Women were having to run the estates and many proved to be very good at it.

The question now arose: what was to be done with all these properties that had once been great castles and hunting lodges? It was obvious that the upkeep was going to be too expensive for many of them and unless they could generate enough revenue for maintenance they would have to be left to decay, the treasures inside having been removed and probably sold.

The king (or his queen) were still demanding fees and taxes. From areas like Rothwell with a manorial court, where land disputes took up most of the time, revenues would be raised in this way.

There was not a lot of money to repair the castle at Rothwell.

Another reason now for the shortage of money was the Wars of the Roses. Men from across the land were being ordered to fight on their lords' behalf and, whereas fighting in France meant some of the lords' tenants didn't have to go, it was almost impossible for anyone to refuse to fight at home.

In July 1454 the Duke of York, now protector of the realm, went north to quell outbreaks of insurrection, but for the country's sake he had to place the pro-Lancastrian Duke of Exeter in the safe keeping of Pontefract *for the good behaviour of his affinity*. It seems Pontefract Castle must still have been in good condition in order to receive such an important personage.

The one good outcome of this situation was that there were fewer lords to argue amongst themselves but, conversely, there were fewer loyal dukes and earls that the king could call upon to raise an army, although all of them were supposed to do so if they were called to serve.

What we now know of as the 'middle classes' were becoming more prosperous. Sheriffs, merchants, gentlemen farmers, reeves, stewards etc., but also soldiers returning from the wars with their spoils. They couldn't afford to buy the large properties that were available but would be able to buy themselves into higher society and marry wealthy women.

What happened to love?

Craftsmen were now employed to improve living conditions, making places more habitable, probably using the building materials taken from dismantled castles.

This is where Roger Hopton came in. He asked permission of the king, probably through the steward at Pontefract, to build a smaller house in the grounds of Rothwell castle.

This eventually became the Manor House ... and the rest is history!!

The grave slab of Roger Hopton, on view at St Cuthbert Church Ackworth. Hopton was responsible for building the second manor house at Rothwell in 1487-89. He died in 1506.

©David Rains 2006

The demolition of Roger Hopton's manor house at Rothwell in 1977.

A fine view over Rothwell millpond towards Roger Hopton's manor house and the remains of the original manor.

15. Archaeological excavations: Rothwell Manor Geophysical survey

Archaeological Background

THERE IS EVIDENCE FOR OCCUPATION on the site at Rothwell for perhaps a millennium and it is this longevity allied with the changing use of the site with time that imparts Rothwell with particular interest.

The Domesday Book records four halls in Rothwell in 1066, one of which is thought to have been on the manor site. Twenty years later: the land has passed into the hands of the de Lacy family. A medieval survey (extant) undertaken in 1341 describes the manorial residence as well as its hunting park, ponds and mills.

A photograph taken in the late 1950's of the old Rothwell Mill and millpond. A mill of some form had been on the site for over 1000 years

West Yorkshire Archaeological Services WYAS was commissioned to carry out a geophysical (earth resistance) survey at Rothwell Manor, a Scheduled Ancient Monument.

The manor is thought to have been divided into a domestic complex to the south-east of the site and a farmyard or agricultural area to the west. Most of the domestic buildings were probably built of stone and are thought to have comprised a manor house with many rooms which lay on an approximate east-west alignment, with a solar to the west of the manor house.

A chapel was situated to the south of the manor house, near to the solar. Service facilities were probably separate from the manor house and would have included a pantry, buttery, kitchen, bake house, larder house, brew house, storehouse, and a long house. All are thought to have been free standing structures in the domestic area.

The agricultural part of the complex included, to the west, a garden which, on its south side was bounded by a hedge, to the north the mill pond.

A barn and a great barn, a stable and a great stable, a cattle shed, a sheepfold and a cottage called the "Smyth", which was located within the garden of the Barn, were probably timber-framed buildings with daubed walls.

In 1341 the eastern boundary was enclosed by stone walls in which a gate was positioned opposite the parish church. A small defensive ditch is likely to have been dug outside the wall, along the eastern edge. To the south a hedge marked the boundary of the manor beyond which a stream powered the mill house.

By the 1480s the house had fallen into extreme disrepair (*in grete ruyine*) and it was granted to Roger Hopton on condition that he built a new house. This new building (Manor Farm) survived until 1977 when it was demolished after having been carefully dismantled and recorded.

Conclusions

The survey has clearly shown that the sub-surface remains of a single building, assumed to be the manorial chapel, survive and that the standing stone column forms the north-east corner of this building.

Additional high resistance anomalies suggest that other walls/buildings are likely to survive close to the surface. Some of these features, although within the scheduled area, are in areas of public access. This may have implications for the future management of the site.

The apparent clarity with which these features can be discerned suggests that most of the stonework above ground level was re-used or taken off site for disposal rather than the buildings be allowed to fall down.

2002

By Dave Weldrake
West Yorkshire Archaeology Service

Trench I (4.5 x 4.0m.]

The area was de-turfed and the topsoil (001) removed to a depth of 0.12m. to reveal a layer of compacted clay with a large number of stones included in the matrix (002). The surface of this layer was scored with several parallel gullies which might represent marks left by the teeth of a JCB bucket. Layer 002 was too compacted to remove effectively with the equipment and workforce which we had available and Trench 1 was abandoned and back-filled. The only finds to be recovered in Trench 1 were modern in origin.

Trench II (9.0 x1.5m.)

The topsoil (011) was removed to a maximum depth of 0.20m. to reveal a hard compacted layer consisting of fragments of stone in a clay matrix (012). A small test pit (approximately 0.75 x 0.75m.) was dug in layer 012 to a depth of 0.30m. As there was no change in the degree of compaction it was decided to abandon Trench II at this point and the excavation was backfilled. No finds were recovered.

Trench III (4.0 x 3.0m.)

The topsoil (021) was removed from this Trench to reveal the surface of a further compacted layer (022) similar in nature to layers 002 and 012. Layer 022 sloped steeply downwards in the southern half of the excavation where it was possible to remove topsoil to a depth of c. 0.60m without reaching a further layer. Removal of layer 021 was not completed due to insufficient time. The only finds to be recovered from Trench III were modern items.

Interpretation

The three trenches excavated showed a marked lack of finds even in the topsoil layers. This is in contrast to excavations where the topsoil has been examined elsewhere in the county (e.g. Weldrake 2001 and 2002).

One would normally expect to find material from night-soiling on agricultural land and its absence, along with the compacted material revealed in all three trenches, is indicative of substantial re-landscaping of the immediate area in the recent past. This would be consistent with levelling of the spoil heaps of Rose Pit to make a public amenity area, but, at the time of the excavation, it was believed that the remade land did not extend as far as the locations of the trenches.

No material relating to the castle or the mill was exposed in Trench I, although it is possible that such remains may still exist below the compacted material. No trace of the anomaly noted on the geophysical survey was observed in either Trench II or III. It is possible that it might lie below the depth to which the excavation could be taken. In either case further work with a mechanical excavator might have proved fruitful.

Illustrating the geophysical survey undertaken in 2002. The lack of recognisable anomalies made the placing of the trenches difficult and yielded no finds of any significance.

2003

By Dave Weldrake
West Yorkshire Archaeology Service

Rothwell Castle *(SE 343 285)*

Rothwell Castle forms an important medieval and post medieval manorial site (Wrathmell 2003), the core of which is now a Scheduled Ancient Monument.

The excavations carried out by the WYAS Advisory Service were part of a much larger Rothwell Castle Project designed to enhance local awareness of this important site. The project as a whole was initiated by the Rothwell and District Historical Society for which they succeeded in obtaining HLF funding. Further support for the excavation work was obtained through the schools' Gifted and Talented funding and through Leeds City Council's 'Breeze' funding.

The object of the investigations was to determine if further buried archaeology remained intact outside the scheduled area. The question remained in doubt since much of the land adjacent to the castle site was graded to form a public amenity access area after the closure of the nearby Rose Pit.

Accordingly, a small L-shaped trench (maximum dimensions 5.0m.) was excavated just to the west of the scheduled area.

Removal of the topsoil revealed a partially cobbled surface which overlay a stone-lined drain in the northern part of the trench. The drain was aligned in a NW-SE direction as if to flow out into Haigh Beck c. 20m. to the south of the site. However, no outflow could be ascertained at, what seemed to be, the appropriate place in the bank of the stream, although other masonry was visible elsewhere.

The drain could not be traced all the way across the trench because of the obscuring layer of cobbles. However, the same alignment was respected by a wall footing immediately to the west of the line of the drain in the south part of the trench.

Dating these features is problematical. The only finds recovered from this site were of 19th and 20th century date and came from the topsoil only. No finds were made in the lower levels. However the stone lined drain is unlikely to be later than the mid 19th century when such features were commonly replaced by the pottery equivalent. (Harvey 1976)

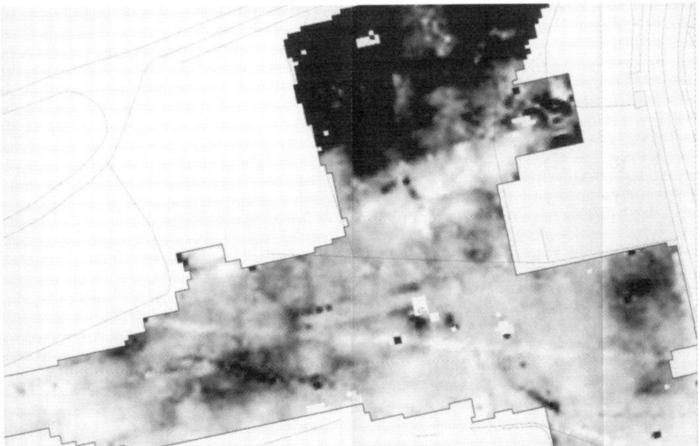

Illustrating the geophysical survey undertaken in 2003, which clearly shows walls and anomalies throughout the scheduled area of manor site.

©West Yorkshire Archaeology Service (WYAS) 2003

2004

By Dave Weldrake
West Yorkshire Archaeology Service

Rothwell Castle *(SE 353 285)*

LAST YEAR'S EXCAVATIONS AT ROTHWELL had revealed part of a wall and, what was thought at the time to be, part of a medieval stone-lined drain. (Weldrake 2004). However, work on site had to be abandoned because of adverse weather conditions before the relationship between the two features could be determined. It was therefore decided to return to the same area to do so.

Last year's trench was therefore reopened, forming an L-shaped excavation (Maximum dimensions 5.0 x 4.5m.).

The trench was re-opened in the final year of archaeological digs on the site in 2004. This was thought to form part of the fortified wall of the manor.

©Eric Wright 2004

Further work established that what were previously considered two features were in fact one. Stones slipping down against the east side of the wall had given the appearance of a drain to one section of the wall . A 5.5m. length of walling was visible within the trench but it clearly extended beyond the limits of the excavation to both the north and the south. Only the eastern face of this structure could be determined with what appeared to be rubble infill to its rear.

This would suggest that the western face of the wall too was beyond the limits of the excavation. The features are clearly of some considerable size and it is conceivable that it might represent the boundary wall of the Rothwell Manor complex.

At the time it was excavated in 2003 this was believed to be a gully drain, but during the dig of 2004 it was thought to be possibly a part of the fortified manor wall.

©West Yorkshire Archaeology Service (WYAS)

The wall was set into a rubble-levelling layer, which was also cut by a number of small pits. One of these immediately adjacent to the wall showed a clear post pipe and may have been intended for a scaffolding post during work on the wall.

The pits contained a variety of finds, including metal-working debris and medieval pottery. This work will be reported on in more detail elsewhere.

Due to constraints of time and resources, little more work has been done on the sequencing of the features noted above. However, Liz Weldrake has analysed the finds. She has identified several indicators of metal working processes amongst them. These include slag and other furnace debris, as well as part of a crucible. Also recovered from the excavation was an intact knife blade 12cm. long.

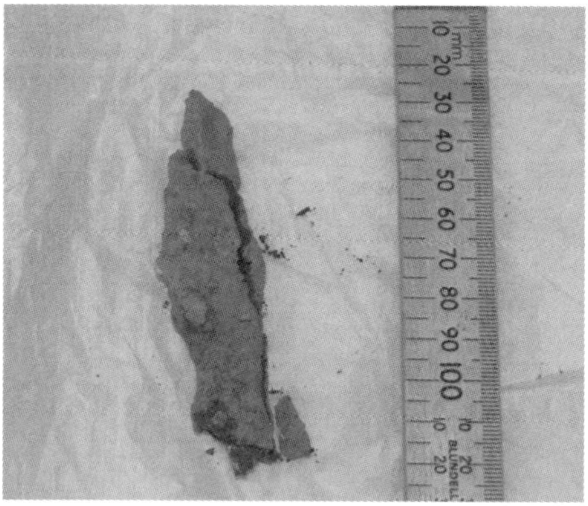

What is believed to be a small knife blade dug up during the 2004 archaeological dig

©West Yorkshire Archaeology Service (WYAS) 2004

Dating the period of this activity is problematic. Victorian pottery has been recovered from some of these features but this may be intrusive. A number of fragments of, what may be, medieval gritty ware was also found, suggesting an earlier date for the metalworking.

My own feeling is that the metalworking debris represents material from a dump which was ‘quarried’ to backfill the pits, rather than being material lying around on the surface which was accidentally incorporated into the backfill. This is confirmed by the absence of large amounts of metal in the layers sealing the pits.

This would suggest there has been metal working in the vicinity of the excavations but not on that exact spot.

If the Victorian pottery is accepted as intrusive, the presence of the gritty ware (possibly 12th century) could point to a medieval date for the metalworking.

This makes the find quite significant, as only one other medieval metalworking site (at Myers Wood, Huddersfield) has been excavated in West Yorkshire.

Dave Weldrake
Education and Outreach Coordinator
West Yorkshire Archaeology Advisory Service

A picturesque view of the pillar of masonry, which is all that is left of the fortified manor house.

Bibliography

Medieval Britain
Lloyd And Jennifer Laing
Herbert Press 1996 Edition
History Of Western Civilisation
Dr, Ellis L Knox
Boise State University Revised July 1995
The Formation of the English Common Law, Norman Conquest to Magna Carta.
John Hudson.
From Catholic to Protestant
Doreen Rosman U.C.L. Press 1996
Medieval England - Rural Society and Economic change 1086-1348
Edward Miller & John Hatcher Longman 1985
The Medieval World
edited by Jaques Le Goff
Parkgate Books 1990
Anglo-Saxon Chronicle 1087 - 1099
The Church in the Middle Ages
Dr M.D. McGee Internet
Rothwell in the 900 years after Domesday
Albert Brown 1987
Notes on the history of the church of the Holy Trinity Rothwell
Issued in connection with the 8th Centenary of the parish church of Rothwell at the request of the vicar, Rev Branscombe, in 1930.
Professor A Hamilton Thompson,
Leeds University.

History of Rothwell
John Batty *1877*
James of Savoy: Welsh Castle Builder?

How would you survive in the Middle Ages?
Fiona Macdonald
Watts Books 1995 edition.
Castle Diary: The journal of Tobias Burgess, page.
Richard Platt
Walker books Ltd. 2001 edition
John of Gaunt: The exercise of Princely Power in Fourteenth Century Europe.
Anthony Goodman
Longman Group, UK Ltd 1992
The Lives of the Kings and Queens of England
Edited by *Antonia Fraser*
Weidenfeld and Nicholson, 1975
The making of Britain: The High Middle Ages 1200-1550
Trevor Rowley
Routledge & Kegan Paul 1986

Articles:
The peasant and agriculture *Giovanni Cherubini*
The Merchant *Aron Ja.Gurevich*

Samantha Letters on line Gazetteer of Markets and fairs in England and Wales to 1516
[Yorkshire] last updated 22nd June 2004-07-21
Lancaster and York. The Wars of the Roses
Alison Weir. Published 1995.

The Wars of the Roses.
Anthony Cheetham.
Edited by *Antonia Fraser*. Published 2000.
Readers Digest.Heritage of Britain. Edition 1975
Marks and Spencer. Kings and Queens.
Joyce Marlow and Elspeth McKay.
Published 1977.
Rothwell: The Medieval Manor and Manorial Mills
S Wrathwell WYAS 2003
Rothwell Manor, Rothwell, West Yorkshire: Geophysical Survey, April 2003
Report No. 1099 © 2003 WYAS
Land adjacent to Rothwell Manor, Rothwell, West Yorkshire: Geophysical Survey, September 2002
Report No. 1042 © 2002 WYAS
Topography and Natural History of Lofthouse and Neighbourhood
George Roberts 1882
Topography and Natural History of Lofthouse and Neighbourhood, vol II
1885
The Three Edwards - War and State in England, 1272 - 1377
Michael Prestwich 1980

Any other publication that has been used to establish historical fact.

Notes

Notes

Notes

Notes

Notes

Notes

Notes